/ 75

The Myth of Sisyphus

and Other Essays

Albert Camus

The Myth of Sisyphus

and Other Essays

Translated from the French by Justin O'Brien

Vintage Books
A Division of Random House
New York

VINTAGE BOOKS

are published by ALFRED A. KNOPF, INC.

and RANDOM HOUSE, INC.

Originally published in France as LE MYTHE DE SISYPHE. Copyright,
1942, by Librairie Gallimard. The other essays have been taken from
various collections of essays by Albert Camus published by Librairie
Gallimard.

Manufactured in the United States of America

Preface

*

For me "The Myth of Sisyphus" marks the beginning of an idea which I was to pursue in The Rebel. It attempts to resolve the problem of suicide, as The Rebel attempts to resolve that of murder, in both cases without the aid of eternal values which, temporarily perhaps, are absent or distorted in contemporary Europe. The fundamental subject of "The Myth of Sisyphus" is this: it is legitimate and necessary to wonder whether life has a meaning; therefore it is legitimate to meet the problem of suicide face to face. The answer, underlying and appearing through the paradoxes which cover it, is this: even if one does not believe in God, suicide is not legitimate. Written fifteen years ago, in 1940, amid the French and European disaster, this book declares that even within the limits of nihilism it is possible to find the means to proceed beyond nihilism. In all the books I have written since, I have attempted to pursue this direction. Although "The Myth of Sisyphus" poses mortal problems, it sums itself up for me as a lucid invitation to live and to create, in the very midst of the desert.

It has hence been thought possible to append to this philosophical argument a series of essays, of a kind I have never ceased writing, which are somewhat marginal to my other books. In a more lyrical form, they all illustrate that essential fluctuation from assent to refusal which, in my view, defines the artist and his difficult calling. The unity of this book, that I should like to be apparent to American readers as it is to me, resides in the reflection, alternately cold and impassioned, in which an artist may indulge as to his reasons for living and for creating. After fifteen years I have progressed beyond several of the positions which are set down here; but I have remained faithful, it seems to me, to the exigency which prompted them. That is why this book is in a certain sense the most personal of those I have published in America. More than the others, therefore, it has need of the indulgence and understanding of its readers.

Albert Camus

Paris, March 1955

Contents

*

The Myth of Sisyphus   1

AN ABSURD REASONING   3

Absurdity and Suicide   3

Absurd Walls   8

Philosophical Suicide   21

Absurd Freedom   38

THE ABSURD MAN   49

Don Juanism   51

Drama   57

Conquest   62

ABSURD CREATION   69

Philosophy and Fiction   69

Kirilov   77

Ephemeral Creation   83

THE MYTH OF SISYPHUS   88

APPENDIX: HOPE AND THE ABSURD IN THE WORK

OF FRANZ KAFKA   92

Summer in Algiers   104

The Minotaur, or The Stop in Oran   114

Helen's Exile   134

Return to Tipasa   139

The Artist and His Time   147

The Myth of Sisyphus

> *O my soul, do not aspire to*
> *immortal life, but exhaust the limits of the possible.*
> PINDAR, *Pythian* iii

The pages that follow deal with an absurd sensitivity that can be found widespread in the age—and not with an absurd philosophy which our time, properly speaking, has not known. It is therefore simply fair to point out, at the outset, what these pages owe to certain contemporary thinkers. It is so far from my intention to hide this that they will be found cited and commented upon throughout this work.

But it is useful to note at the same time that the absurd, hitherto taken as a conclusion, is considered in this essay as a starting-point. In this sense it may be said that there is something provisional in my commentary: one cannot prejudge the position it entails. There will be found here merely the description, in the pure state, of an intellectual malady. No metaphysic, no belief is involved in it for the moment. These are the limits and the only bias of this book. Certain personal experiences urge me to make this clear.

An Absurd Reasoning

Absurdity and Suicide

There is but one truly serious philosophical problem, and that is suicide. Judging whether life is or is not worth living amounts to answering the fundamental question of philosophy. All the rest—whether or not the world has three dimensions, whether the mind has nine or twelve categories—comes afterwards. These are games; one must first answer. And if it is true, as Nietzsche claims, that a philosopher, to deserve our respect, must preach by example, you can appreciate the importance of that reply, for it will precede the definitive act. These are facts the heart can feel; yet they call for careful study before they become clear to the intellect.

If I ask myself how to judge that this question is more urgent than that, I reply that one judges by the actions it entails. I have never seen anyone die for the ontological argument. Galileo, who held a scientific truth of great importance, abjured it with the greatest ease as soon as it endangered his life. In a certain sense, he did right.[1] That truth was not worth the stake. Whether the earth or the sun revolves around the other is a matter of profound indifference. To tell the truth, it is a futile question. On the other hand, I see many people die because they judge

[1] From the point of view of the relative value of truth. On the other hand, from the point of view of virile behavior, this scholar's fragility may well make us smile.

that life is not worth living. I see others paradoxically getting killed for the ideas or illusions that give them a reason for living (what is called a reason for living is also an excellent reason for dying). I therefore conclude that the meaning of life is the most urgent of questions. How to answer it? On all essential problems (I mean thereby those that run the risk of leading to death or those that intensify the passion of living) there are probably but two methods of thought: the method of La Palisse and the method of Don Quixote. Solely the balance between evidence and lyricism can allow us to achieve simultaneously emotion and lucidity. In a subject at once so humble and so heavy with emotion, the learned and classical dialectic must yield, one can see, to a more modest attitude of mind deriving at one and the same time from common sense and understanding.

Suicide has never been dealt with except as a social phenomenon. On the contrary, we are concerned here, at the outset, with the relationship between individual thought and suicide. An act like this is prepared within the silence of the heart, as is a great work of art. The man himself is ignorant of it. One evening he pulls the trigger or jumps. Of an apartment-building manager who had killed himself I was told that he had lost his daughter five years before, that he had changed greatly since, and that that experience had "undermined" him. A more exact word cannot be imagined. Beginning to think is beginning to be undermined. Society has but little connection with such beginnings. The worm is in man's heart. That is where it must be sought. One must follow and understand this fatal game that leads from lucidity in the face of existence to flight from light.

There are many causes for a suicide, and generally the most obvious ones were not the most powerful. Rarely is suicide committed (yet the hypothesis is not excluded) through reflection. What sets off the crisis is almost always unverifiable. Newspapers often speak of "personal sorrows" or of "incurable illness." These explanations are plausible. But one would have to know whether a friend of the desperate man had not that very day addressed him indifferently. He is the guilty one. For that is enough to precipitate all the rancors and all the boredom still in suspension.[2]

But if it is hard to fix the precise instant, the subtle step when the mind opted for death, it is easier to deduce from the act itself the consequences it implies. In a sense, and as in melodrama, killing yourself amounts to confessing. It is confessing that life is too much for you or that you do not understand it. Let's not go too far in such analogies, however, but rather return to everyday words. It is merely confessing that that "is not worth the trouble." Living, naturally, is never easy. You continue making the gestures commanded by existence for many reasons, the first of which is habit. Dying voluntarily implies that you have recognized, even instinctively, the ridiculous character of that habit, the absence of any profound reason for living, the insane character of that daily agitation, and the uselessness of suffering.

What, then, is that incalculable feeling that deprives the mind of the sleep necessary to life? A world that can be explained even with bad reasons is a familiar world. But, on the other hand, in a universe suddenly divested of illusions and lights, man feels an alien, a stranger. His exile is without remedy since he is deprived of the memory of a lost home or the hope of a promised land. This divorce between man and his life, the actor and his setting, is properly the feeling of absurdity. All healthy men having thought of their own suicide, it can be seen, without further explanation, that there is a direct connection between this feeling and the longing for death.

The subject of this essay is precisely this relationship between the absurd and suicide, the exact degree to which suicide is a solution to the absurd. The principle can be established that for a man who does not cheat, what he believes to be true must determine his action. Belief in the absurdity of existence must then dictate his conduct. It is legitimate to wonder, clearly and without false pathos, whether a conclusion of this importance requires forsaking

[2] Let us not miss this opportunity to point out the relative character of this essay. Suicide may indeed be related to much more honorable considerations—for example, the political suicides of protest, as they were called, during the Chinese revolution.

as rapidly as possible an incomprehensible condition. I am speaking, of course, of men inclined to be in harmony with themselves.

Stated clearly, this problem may seem both simple and insoluble. But it is wrongly assumed that simple questions involve answers that are no less simple and that evidence implies evidence. A *priori* and reversing the terms of the problem, just as one does or does not kill oneself, it seems that there are but two philosophical solutions, either yes or no. This would be too easy. But allowance must be made for those who, without concluding, continue questioning. Here I am only slightly indulging in irony: this is the majority. I notice also that those who answer "no" act as if they thought "yes." As a matter of fact, if I accept the Nietzschean criterion, they think "yes" in one way or another. On the other hand, it often happens that those who commit suicide were assured of the meaning of life. These contradictions are constant. It may even be said that they have never been so keen as on this point where, on the contrary, logic seems so desirable. It is a commonplace to compare philosophical theories and the behavior of those who profess them. But it must be said that of the thinkers who refused a meaning to life none except Kirilov who belongs to literature, Peregrinos who is born of legend,[3] and Jules Lequier who belongs to hypothesis, admitted his logic to the point of refusing that life. Schopenhauer is often cited, as a fit subject for laughter, because he praised suicide while seated at a well-set table. This is no subject for joking. That way of not taking the tragic seriously is not so grievous, but it helps to judge a man.

In the face of such contradictions and obscurities must we conclude that there is no relationship between the opinion one has about life and the act one commits to leave it? Let us not exaggerate in this direction. In a man's attachment to life there is something stronger than all the ills in the world. The body's judgment is as good as the mind's, and the body shrinks from annihilation.

---

[3] I have heard of an emulator of Peregrinos, a post-war writer who, after having finished his first book, committed suicide to attract attention to his work. Attention was in fact attracted, but the book was judged no good.

We get into the habit of living before acquiring the habit of thinking. In that race which daily hastens us toward death, the body maintains its irreparable lead. In short, the essence of that contradiction lies in what I shall call the act of eluding because it is both less and more than diversion in the Pascalian sense. Eluding is the invariable game. The typical act of eluding, the fatal evasion that constitutes the third theme of this essay, is hope. Hope of another life one must "deserve" or trickery of those who live not for life itself but for some great idea that will transcend it, refine it, give it a meaning, and betray it.

Thus everything contributes to spreading confusion. Hitherto, and it has not been wasted effort, people have played on words and pretended to believe that refusing to grant a meaning to life necessarily leads to declaring that it is not worth living. In truth, there is no necessary common measure between these two judgments. One merely has to refuse to be misled by the confusions, divorces, and inconsistencies previously pointed out. One must brush everything aside and go straight to the real problem. One kills oneself because life is not worth living, that is certainly a truth—yet an unfruitful one because it is a truism. But does that insult to existence, that flat denial in which it is plunged come from the fact that it has no meaning? Does its absurdity require one to escape it through hope or suicide—this is what must be clarified, hunted down, and elucidated while brushing aside all the rest. Does the Absurd dictate death? This problem must be given priority over others, outside all methods of thought and all exercises of the disinterested mind. Shades of meaning, contradictions, the psychology that an "objective" mind can always introduce into all problems have no place in this pursuit and this passion. It calls simply for an unjust—in other words, logical—thought. That is not easy. It is always easy to be logical. It is almost impossible to be logical to the bitter end. Men who die by their own hand consequently follow to its conclusion their emotional inclination. Reflection on suicide gives me an opportunity to raise the only problem to interest me: is there a logic to the point of death? I cannot know unless I pursue, without reckless passion, in the sole light of evidence, the reasoning of which I am here suggesting the source. This is what I call an absurd reasoning. Many have begun it. I do not yet know whether or not they kept to it.

When Karl Jaspers, revealing the impossibility of constituting the world as a unity, exclaims: "This limitation leads me to myself, where I can no longer withdraw behind an objective point of view that I am merely representing, where neither I myself nor the existence of others can any longer become an object for me," he is evoking after many others those waterless deserts where thought reaches its confines. After many others, yes indeed, but how eager they were to get out of them! At that last crossroad where thought hesitates, many men have arrived and even some of the humblest. They then abdicated what was most precious to them, their life. Others, princes of the mind, abdicated likewise, but they initiated the suicide of their thought in its purest revolt. The real effort is to stay there, rather, in so far as that is possible, and to examine closely the odd vegetation of those distant regions. Tenacity and acumen are privileged spectators of this inhuman show in which absurdity, hope, and death carry on their dialogue. The mind can then analyze the figures of that elementary yet subtle dance before illustrating them and reliving them itself.

Absurd Walls

Like great works, deep feelings always mean more than they are conscious of saying. The regularity of an impulse or a repulsion in a soul is encountered again in habits of doing or thinking, is reproduced in consequences of which the soul itself knows nothing. Great feelings take with them their own universe, splendid or abject. They light up with their passion an exclusive world in which they recognize their climate. There is a universe of jealousy, of ambition, of selfishness, or of generosity. A universe—in other words, a metaphysic and an attitude of mind. What is true of already specialized feelings will be even more so of emotions basically as indeterminate, simultaneously as vague and as "definite," as remote and as "present" as those furnished us by beauty or aroused by absurdity.

At any streetcorner the feeling of absurdity can strike any man in the face. As it is, in its distressing nudity, in its light without effulgence, it is elusive. But that very difficulty deserves reflection. It is probably true that a man remains forever unknown to us and that there is in him something irreducible that escapes us. But *practically* I know men and recognize them by their behavior, by the totality of their deeds, by the consequences caused in life by their presence. Likewise, all those irrational feelings which offer no purchase to analysis. I can define them *practically*, appreciate them *practically*, by gathering together the sum of their consequences in the domain of the intelligence, by seizing and noting all their aspects, by outlining their universe. It is certain that apparently, though I have seen the same actor a hundred times, I shall not for that reason know him any better personally. Yet if I add up the heroes he has personified and if I say that I know him a little better at the hundredth character counted off, this will be felt to contain an element of truth. For this apparent paradox is also an apologue. There is a moral to it. It teaches that a man defines himself by his make-believe as well as by his sincere impulses. There is thus a lower key of feelings, inaccessible in the heart but partially disclosed by the acts they imply and the attitudes of mind they assume. It is clear that in this way I am defining a method. But it is also evident that that method is one of analysis and not of knowledge. For methods imply metaphysics; unconsciously they disclose conclusions that they often claim not to know yet. Similarly, the last pages of a book are already contained in the first pages. Such a link is inevitable. The method defined here acknowledges the feeling that all true knowledge is impossible. Solely appearances can be enumerated and the climate make itself felt.

Perhaps we shall be able to overtake that elusive feeling of absurdity in the different but closely related worlds of intelligence, of the art of living, or of art itself. The climate of absurdity is in the beginning. The end is the absurd universe and that attitude of mind which lights the world with its true colors to bring out the privileged and implacable visage which that attitude has discerned in it.

All great deeds and all great thoughts have a ridiculous beginning. Great works are often born on a street-corner or in a restaurant's revolving door. So it is with absurdity. The absurd world more than others derives its nobility from that abject birth. In certain situations, replying "nothing" when asked what one is thinking about may be pretense in a man. Those who are loved are well aware of this. But if that reply is sincere, if it symbolizes that odd state of soul in which the void becomes eloquent, in which the chain of daily gestures is broken, in which the heart vainly seeks the link that will connect it again, then it is as it were the first sign of absurdity.

It happens that the stage sets collapse. Rising, street-car, four hours in the office or the factory, meal, streetcar, four hours of work, meal, sleep, and Monday Tuesday Wednesday Thursday Friday and Saturday according to the same rhythm—this path is easily followed most of the time. But one day the "why" arises and everything begins in that weariness tinged with amazement. "Begins"—this is important. Weariness comes at the end of the acts of a mechanical life, but at the same time it inaugurates the impulse of consciousness. It awakens consciousness and provokes what follows. What follows is the gradual return into the chain or it is the definitive awakening. At the end of the awakening comes, in time, the consequence: suicide or recovery. In itself weariness has something sickening about it. Here, I must conclude that it is good. For everything begins with consciousness and nothing is worth anything except through it. There is nothing original about these remarks. But they are obvious; that is enough for a while, during a sketchy reconnaissance in the origins of the absurd. Mere "anxiety," as Heidegger says, is at the source of everything.

Likewise and during every day of an unillustrious life, time carries us. But a moment always comes when we have to carry it. We live on the future: "tomorrow," "later on," "when you have made your way," "you will understand when you are old enough." Such irrelevancies are wonderful, for, after all, it's a matter of dying. Yet a day comes when a man notices or says that he is thirty. Thus he asserts his youth. But simultaneously he situates himself in relation to time. He takes his place in it. He admits that he stands at a certain point on a curve that he acknowledges having to travel to its end. He belongs to time, and by the horror that seizes him, he recognizes his worst enemy. Tomorrow, he was longing for tomorrow, whereas everything in him ought to reject it. That revolt of the flesh is the absurd.[4]

A step lower and strangeness creeps in: perceiving that the world is "dense," sensing to what a degree a stone is foreign and irreducible to us, with what intensity nature or a landscape can negate us. At the heart of all beauty lies something inhuman, and these hills, the softness of the sky, the outline of these trees at this very minute lose the illusory meaning with which we had clothed them, henceforth more remote than a lost paradise. The primitive hostility of the world rises up to face us across millennia. For a second we cease to understand it because for centuries we have understood in it solely the images and designs that we had attributed to it beforehand, because henceforth we lack the power to make use of that artifice. The world evades us because it becomes itself again. That stage scenery masked by habit becomes again what it is. It withdraws at a distance from us. Just as there are days when under the familiar face of a woman, we see as a stranger her we had loved months or years ago, perhaps we shall come even to desire what suddenly leaves us so alone. But the time has not yet come. Just one thing: that denseness and that strangeness of the world is the absurd.

Men, too, secrete the inhuman. At certain moments of lucidity, the mechanical aspect of their gestures, their meaningless pantomime makes silly everything that surrounds them. A man is talking on the telephone behind a glass partition; you cannot hear him, but you see his incomprehensible dumb show: you wonder why he is alive. This discomfort in the face of man's own inhumanity, this incalculable tumble before the image of what we are, this "nausea," as a writer of today calls it, is also the absurd. Likewise the stranger who at certain seconds comes to meet us in a mirror, the familiar and yet alarming brother we encounter in our own photographs is also the absurd.

---

[4] But not in the proper sense. This is not a definition, but rather an *enumeration* of the feelings that may admit of the absurd. Still, the enumeration finished, the absurd has nevertheless not been exhausted.

I come at last to death and to the attitude we have toward it. On this point everything has been said and it is only proper to avoid pathos. Yet one will never be sufficiently surprised that everyone lives as if no one "knew." This is because in reality there is no experience of death. Properly speaking, nothing has been experienced but what has been lived and made conscious. Here, it is barely possible to speak of the experience of others' deaths. It is a substitute, an illusion, and it never quite convinces us. That melancholy convention cannot be persuasive. The horror comes in reality from the mathematical aspect of the event. If time frightens us, this is because it works out the problem and the solution comes afterward. All the pretty speeches about the soul will have their contrary convincingly proved, at least for a time. From this inert body on which a slap makes no mark the soul has disappeared. This elementary and definitive aspect of the adventure constitutes the absurd feeling. Under the fatal lighting of that destiny, its uselessness becomes evident. No code of ethics and no effort are justifiable *a priori* in the face of the cruel mathematics that command our condition.

Let me repeat: all this has been said over and over. I am limiting myself here to making a rapid classification and to pointing out these obvious themes. They run through all literatures and all philosophies. Everyday conversation feeds on them. There is no question of reinventing them. But it is essential to be sure of these facts in order to be able to question oneself subsequently on the primordial question. I am interested—let me repeat again —not so much in absurd discoveries as in their consequences. If one is assured of these facts, what is one to conclude, how far is one to go to elude nothing? Is one to die voluntarily or to hope in spite of everything? Beforehand, it is necessary to take the same rapid inventory on the plane of the intelligence.

The mind's first step is to distinguish what is true from what is false. However, as soon as thought reflects on itself, what it first discovers is a contradiction. Useless to strive to be convincing in this case. Over the centuries no one has furnished a clearer and more elegant demonstration of the business than Aristotle: "The often ridiculed consequence of these opinions is that they destroy themselves. For by asserting that all is true we assert the truth of the contrary assertion and consequently the falsity of our own thesis (for the contrary assertion does not admit that it can be true). And if one says that all is false, that assertion is itself false. If we declare that solely the assertion opposed to ours is false or else that solely ours is not false, we are nevertheless forced to admit an infinite number of true or false judgments. For the one who expresses a true assertion proclaims simultaneously that it is true, and so on *ad infinitum*."

This vicious circle is but the first of a series in which the mind that studies itself gets lost in a giddy whirling. The very simplicity of these paradoxes makes them irreducible. Whatever may be the plays on words and the acrobatics of logic, to understand is, above all, to unify. The mind's deepest desire, even in its most elaborate operations, parallels man's unconscious feeling in the face of his universe: it is an insistence upon familiarity, an appetite for clarity. Understanding the world for a man is reducing it to the human, stamping it with his seal. The cat's universe is not the universe of the anthill. The truism "All thought is anthropomorphic" has no other meaning. Likewise, the mind that aims to understand reality can consider itself satisfied only by reducing it to terms of thought. If man realized that the universe like him can love and suffer, he would be reconciled. If thought discovered in the shimmering mirrors of phenomena eternal relations capable of summing them up and summing themselves up in a single principle, then would be seen an intellectual joy of which the myth of the blessed would be but a ridiculous imitation. That nostalgia for unity, that appetite for the absolute illustrates the essential impulse of the human drama. But the fact of that nostalgia's existence does not imply that it is to be immediately satisfied. For if, bridging the gulf that separates desire from conquest, we assert with Parmenides the reality of the One (whatever it may be), we fall into the ridiculous contradiction of a mind that asserts total unity and proves by its very assertion its own difference and the diversity it claimed to resolve. This other vicious circle is enough to stifle our hopes.

These are again truisms. I shall again repeat that they are not interesting in themselves but in the consequences that can be deduced from them. I know another truism: it tells me that man is mortal. One can nevertheless count the minds that have deduced the extreme conclusions from it. It is essential to consider as a constant point of reference in this essay the regular hiatus between what we fancy we know and what we really know, practical assent and simulated ignorance which allows us to live with ideas which, if we truly put them to the test, ought to upset our whole life. Faced with this inextricable contradiction of the mind, we shall fully grasp the divorce separating us from our own creations. So long as the mind keeps silent in the motionless world of its hopes, everything is reflected and arranged in the unity of its nostalgia. But with its first move this world cracks and tumbles: an infinite number of shimmering fragments is offered to the understanding. We must despair of ever reconstructing the familiar, calm surface which would give us peace of heart. After so many centuries of inquiries, so many abdications among thinkers, we are well aware that this is true for all our knowledge. With the exception of professional rationalists, today people despair of true knowledge. If the only significant history of human thought were to be written, it would have to be the history of its successive regrets and its impotences.

Of whom and of what indeed can I say: "I know that!" This heart within me I can feel, and I judge that it exists. This world I can touch, and I likewise judge that it exists. There ends all my knowledge, and the rest is construction. For if I try to seize this self of which I feel sure, if I try to define and to summarize it, it is nothing but water slipping through my fingers. I can sketch one by one all the aspects it is able to assume, all those likewise that have been attributed to it, this upbringing, this origin, this ardor or these silences, this nobility or this vileness. But aspects cannot be added up. This very heart which is mine will forever remain indefinable to me. Between the certainty I have of my existence and the content

I try to give to that assurance, the gap will never be filled. Forever I shall be a stranger to myself. In psychology as in logic, there are truths but no truth. Socrates' "Know thyself" has as much value as the "Be virtuous" of our confessionals. They reveal a nostalgia at the same time as an ignorance. They are sterile exercises on great subjects. They are legitimate only in precisely so far as they are approximate.

And here are trees and I know their gnarled surface, water and I feel its taste. These scents of grass and stars at night, certain evenings when the heart relaxes—how shall I negate this world whose power and strength I feel? Yet all the knowledge on earth will give me nothing to assure me that this world is mine. You describe it to me and you teach me to classify it. You enumerate its laws and in my thirst for knowledge I admit that they are true. You take apart its mechanism and my hope increases. At the final stage you teach me that this wondrous and multicolored universe can be reduced to the atom and that the atom itself can be reduced to the electron. All this is good and I wait for you to continue. But you tell me of an invisible planetary system in which electrons gravitate around a nucleus. You explain this world to me with an image. I realize then that you have been reduced to poetry: I shall never know. Have I the time to become indignant? You have already changed theories. So that science that was to teach me everything ends up in a hypothesis, that lucidity founders in metaphor, that uncertainty is resolved in a work of art. What need had I of so many efforts? The soft lines of these hills and the hand of evening on this troubled heart teach me much more. I have returned to my beginning. I realize that if through science I can seize phenomena and enumerate them, I cannot, for all that, apprehend the world. Were I to trace its entire relief with my finger, I should not know any more. And you give me the choice between a description that is sure but that teaches me nothing and hypotheses that claim to teach me but that are not sure. A stranger to myself and to the world, armed solely with a thought that negates itself as soon as it asserts, what is this condition in which I can have peace only by refusing to know and to live, in which the appetite for conquest bumps into walls that defy its assaults? To will is to stir up paradoxes. Everything is ordered in such a way as to bring into being that poisoned peace produced by thoughtlessness, lack of heart, or fatal renunciations.

Hence the intelligence, too, tells me in its way that this world is absurd. Its contrary, blind reason, may well claim that all is clear; I was waiting for proof and longing for it to be right. But despite so many pretentious centuries and over the heads of so many eloquent and persuasive men, I know that is false. On this plane, at least, there is no happiness if I cannot know. That universal reason, practical or ethical, that determinism, those categories that explain everything are enough to make a decent man laugh. They have nothing to do with the mind. They negate its profound truth, which is to be enchained. In this unintelligible and limited universe, man's fate henceforth assumes its meaning. A horde of irrationals has sprung up and surrounds him until his ultimate end. In his recovered and now studied lucidity, the feeling of the absurd becomes clear and definite. I said that the world is absurd, but I was too hasty. This world in itself is not reasonable, that is all that can be said. But what is absurd is the confrontation of this irrational and the wild longing for clarity whose call echoes in the human heart. The absurd depends as much on man as on the world. For the moment it is all that links them together. It binds them one to the other as only hatred can weld two creatures together. This is all I can discern clearly in this measureless universe where my adventure takes place. Let us pause here. If I hold to be true that absurdity that determines my relationship with life, if I become thoroughly imbued with that sentiment that seizes me in face of the world's scenes, with that lucidity imposed on me by the pursuit of a science, I must sacrifice everything to these certainties and I must see them squarely to be able to maintain them. Above all, I must adapt my behavior to them and pursue them in all their consequences. I am speaking here of decency. But I want to know beforehand if thought can live in those deserts.

I already know that thought has at least entered those deserts. There it found its bread. There it realized that it had previously been feeding on phantoms. It justified some of the most urgent themes of human reflection.

From the moment absurdity is recognized, it becomes a passion, the most harrowing of all. But whether or not one can live with one's passions, whether or not one can accept their law, which is to burn the heart they simultaneously exalt—that is the whole question. It is not, however, the one we shall ask just yet. It stands at the center of this experience. There will be time to come back to it. Let us recognize rather those themes and those impulses born of the desert. It will suffice to enumerate them. They, too, are known to all today. There have always been men to defend the rights of the irrational. The tradition of what may be called humiliated thought has never ceased to exist. The criticism of rationalism has been made so often that it seems unnecessary to begin again. Yet our epoch is marked by the rebirth of those paradoxical systems that strive to trip up the reason as if truly it had always forged ahead. But that is not so much a proof of the efficacy of the reason as of the intensity of its hopes. On the plane of history, such a constancy of two attitudes illustrates the essential passion of man torn between his urge toward unity and the clear vision he may have of the walls enclosing him.

But never perhaps at any time has the attack on reason been more violent than in ours. Since Zarathustra's great outburst: "By chance it is the oldest nobility in the world. I conferred it upon all things when I proclaimed that above them no eternal will was exercised," since Kierkegaard's fatal illness, "that malady that leads to death with nothing else following it," the significant and tormenting themes of absurd thought have followed one another. Or at least, and this proviso is of capital importance, the themes of irrational and religious thought. From Jaspers to Heidegger, from Kierkegaard to Chestov, from the phenomenologists to Scheler, on the logical plane and on the moral plane, a whole family of minds related by their nostalgia but opposed by their methods or their aims, have persisted in blocking the royal road of reason and in recovering the direct paths of truth. Here I assume these thoughts to be known and lived. Whatever may be or have been their ambitions, all started out from that indescribable universe where contradiction, antinomy, anguish, or impotence reigns. And what they have in common is precisely the themes so far disclosed. For them, too, it must be said that what matters above all is the conclusions they have managed to draw from those discoveries. That matters so much that they must be examined separately. But for the moment we are concerned solely with their discoveries and their initial experiments. We are concerned solely with noting their agreement. If it would be presumptuous to try to deal with their philosophies, it is possible and sufficient in any case to bring out the climate that is common to them.

Heidegger considers the human condition coldly and announces that that existence is humiliated. The only reality is "anxiety" in the whole chain of beings. To the man lost in the world and its diversions this anxiety is a brief, fleeting fear. But if that fear becomes conscious of itself, it becomes anguish, the perpetual climate of the lucid man "in whom existence is concentrated." This professor of philosophy writes without trembling and in the most abstract language in the world that "the finite and limited character of human existence is more primordial than man himself." His interest in Kant extends only to recognizing the restricted character of his "pure Reason." This is to conclude at the end of his analyses that "the world can no longer offer anything to the man filled with anguish." This anxiety seems to him so much more important than all the categories in the world that he thinks and talks only of it. He enumerates its aspects: boredom when the ordinary man strives to quash it in him and benumb it; terror when the mind contemplates death. He too does not separate consciousness from the absurd. The consciousness of death is the call of anxiety and "existence then delivers itself its own summons through the intermediary of consciousness." It is the very voice of anguish and it adjures existence "to return from its loss in the anonymous They." For him, too, one must not sleep, but must keep alert until the consummation. He stands in this absurd world and points out its ephemeral character. He seeks his way amid these ruins.

Jaspers despairs of any ontology because he claims that we have lost "naïveté." He knows that we can achieve nothing that will transcend the fatal game of appearances. He knows that the end of the mind is failure. He tarries over the spiritual adventures revealed by history and pitilessly discloses the flaw in each system, the illusion that saved everything, the preaching that hid nothing. In this ravaged world in which the impossibility of knowledge is established, in which everlasting nothingness seems the only reality and irremediable despair seems the only attitude, he tries to recover the Ariadne's thread that leads to divine secrets.

Chestov, for his part, throughout a wonderfully monotonous work, constantly straining toward the same truths, tirelessly demonstrates that the tightest system, the most universal rationalism always stumbles eventually on the irrational of human thought. None of the ironic facts or ridiculous contradictions that depreciate the reason escapes him. One thing only interests him, and that is the exception, whether in the domain of the heart or of the mind. Through the Dostoevskian experiences of the condemned man, the exacerbated adventures of the Nietzschean mind, Hamlet's imprecations, or the bitter aristocracy of an Ibsen, he tracks down, illuminates, and magnifies the human revolt against the irremediable. He refuses the reason its reasons and begins to advance with some decision only in the middle of that colorless desert where all certainties have become stones.

Of all perhaps the most engaging, Kierkegaard, for a part of his existence at least, does more than discover the absurd, he lives it. The man who writes: "The surest of stubborn silences is not to hold one's tongue but to talk" makes sure in the beginning that no truth is absolute or can render satisfactory an existence that is impossible in itself. Don Juan of the understanding, he multiplies pseudonyms and contradictions, writes his *Discourses of Edification* at the same time as that manual of cynical spiritualism, *The Diary of the Seducer*. He refuses consolations, ethics, reliable principles. As for that thorn he feels in his heart, he is careful not to quiet its pain. On the contrary, he awakens it and, in the desperate joy of a man crucified and happy to be so, he builds up piece by piece—lucidity, refusal, make-believe—a category of the man possessed. That face both tender and sneering, those pirouettes followed by a cry from the heart are the absurd spirit itself grappling with a reality beyond its comprehension. And the spiritual adventure that leads Kierkegaard to his beloved scandals begins likewise in the chaos of an experience divested of its setting and relegated to its original incoherence.

On quite a different plane, that of method, Husserl and the phenomenologists, by their very extravagances, reinstate the world in its diversity and deny the transcendent power of the reason. The spiritual universe becomes incalculably enriched through them. The rose petal, the milestone, or the human hand are as important as love, desire, or the laws of gravity. Thinking ceases to be unifying or making a semblance familiar in the guise of a major principle. Thinking is learning all over again to see, to be attentive, to focus consciousness; it is turning every idea and every image, in the manner of Proust, into a privileged moment. What justifies thought is its extreme consciousness. Though more positive than Kierkegaard's or Chestov's, Husserl's manner of proceeding, in the beginning, nevertheless negates the classic method of the reason, disappoints hope, opens to intuition and to the heart a whole proliferation of phenomena, the wealth of which has about it something inhuman. These paths lead to all sciences or to none. This amounts to saying that in this case the means are more important than the end. All that is involved is "an attitude for understanding" and not a consolation. Let me repeat: in the beginning, at very least.

How can one fail to feel the basic relationship of these minds! How can one fail to see that they take their stand around a privileged and bitter moment in which hope has no further place? I want everything to be explained to me or nothing. And the reason is impotent when it hears this cry from the heart. The mind aroused by this insistence seeks and finds nothing but contradictions and nonsense. What I fail to understand is nonsense. The world is peopled with such irrationals. The world itself, whose single meaning I do not understand, is but a vast irrational. If one could only say just once: "This is clear," all would be saved. But these men vie with one another in proclaiming that nothing is clear, all is chaos, that all man has is his lucidity and his definite knowledge of the walls surrounding him.

All these experiences agree and confirm one another. The mind, when it reaches its limits, must make a judgment and choose its conclusions. This is where suicide and the reply stand. But I wish to reverse the order of the inquiry and start out from the intelligent adventure and come back to daily acts. The experiences called to mind here were born in the desert that we must not leave behind. A least it is essential to know how far they went. At this point of his effort man stands face to face with the irrational. He feels within him his longing for happiness and for reason. The absurd is born of this confrontation between the human need and the unreasonable silence of the world. This must not be forgotten. This must be clung to because the whole consequence of a life can depend on it. The irrational, the human nostalgia, and the absurd that is born of their encounter— these are the three characters in the drama that must necessarily end with all the logic of which an existence is capable.

Philosophical Suicide

The feeling of the absurd is not, for all that, the notion of the absurd. It lays the foundations for it, and that is all. It is not limited to that notion, except in the brief moment when it passes judgment on the universe. Subsequently it has a chance of going further. It is alive; in other words, it must die or else reverberate. So it is with the themes we have gathered together. But there again what interests me is not works or minds, criticism of which would call for another form and another place, but the discovery of what their conclusions have in common. Never, perhaps, have minds been so different. And yet we recognize as identical the spiritual landscapes in which they get under way. Likewise, despite such dissimilar zones of knowledge, the cry that terminates their itinerary rings out in the same way. It is evident that the thinkers we have just recalled have a common climate.

To say that that climate is deadly scarcely amounts to playing on words. Living under that stifling sky forces one to get away or to stay. The important thing is to find out how people get away in the first case and why people stay in the second case. This is how I define the problem of suicide and the possible interest in the conclusions of existential philosophy.

But first I want to detour from the direct path. Up to now we have managed to circumscribe the absurd from the outside. One can, however, wonder how much is clear in that notion and by direct analysis try to discover its meaning on the one hand and, on the other, the consequences it involves.

If I accuse an innocent man of a monstrous crime, if I tell a virtuous man that he has coveted his own sister, he will reply that this is absurd. His indignation has its comical aspect. But it also has its fundamental reason. The virtuous man illustrates by that reply the definitive antinomy existing between the deed I am attributing to him and his lifelong principles. "It's absurd" means "It's impossible" but also "It's contradictory." If I see a man armed only with a sword attack a group of machine guns, I shall consider his act to be absurd. But it is so solely by virtue of the disproportion between his intention and the reality he will encounter, of the contradiction I notice between his true strength and the aim he has in view. Likewise we shall deem a verdict absurd when we contrast it with the verdict the facts apparently dictated. And, similarly, a demonstration by the absurd is achieved by comparing the consequences of such a reasoning with the logical reality one wants to set up. In all these cases, from the simplest to the most complex, the magnitude of the absurdity will be in direct ratio to the distance between the two terms of my comparison. There are absurd marriages, challenges, rancors, silences, wars, and even peace treaties. For each of them the absurdity springs from a comparison. I am thus justified in saying that the feeling of absurdity does not spring from the mere scrutiny of a fact or an impression, but that it bursts from the comparison between a bare fact and a certain reality, between an action and the world that transcends it. The absurd is essentially a divorce. It lies in neither of the elements compared; it is born of their confrontation.

In this particular case and on the plane of intelligence, I can therefore say that the Absurd is not in man (if such a metaphor could have a meaning) nor in the world, but in their presence together. For the moment it is the only bond uniting them. If I wish to limit myself to facts, I know what man wants, I know what the world offers him, and now I can say that I also know what links them. I have no need to dig deeper. A single certainty is enough for the seeker. He simply has to derive all the consequences from it.

The immediate consequence is also a rule of method. The odd trinity brought to light in this way is certainly not a startling discovery. But it resembles the data of experience in that it is both infinitely simple and infinitely complicated. Its first distinguishing feature in this regard is that it cannot be divided. To destroy one of its terms is to destroy the whole. There can be no absurd outside the human mind. Thus, like everything else, the absurd ends with death. But there can be no absurd outside this world either. And it is by this elementary criterion that I judge the notion of the absurd to be essential and consider that it can stand as the first of my truths. The rule of method alluded to above appears here. If I judge that a thing is true, I must preserve it. If I attempt to solve a problem, at least I must not by that very solution conjure away one of the terms of the problem. For me the sole datum is the absurd. The first and, after all, the only condition of my inquiry is to preserve the very thing that crushes me, consequently to respect what I consider essential in it. I have just defined it as a confrontation and an unceasing struggle.

And carrying this absurd logic to its conclusion, I must admit that that struggle implies a total absence of hope (which has nothing to do with despair), a continual rejection (which must not be confused with renunciation), and a conscious dissatisfaction (which must not be compared to immature unrest). Everything that destroys, conjures away, or exorcises these requirements (and, to begin with, consent which overthrows divorce) ruins the absurd and devaluates the attitude that may then be proposed. The absurd has meaning only in so far as it is not agreed to.

There exists an obvious fact that seems utterly moral: namely, that a man is always a prey to his truths. Once he has admitted them, he cannot free himself from them. One has to pay something. A man who has become conscious of the absurd is forever bound to it. A man devoid of hope and conscious of being so has ceased to belong to the future. That is natural. But it is just as natural that he should strive to escape the universe of which he is the creator. All the foregoing has significance only on account of this paradox. Certain men, starting from a critique of rationalism, have admitted the absurd climate. Nothing is more instructive in this regard than to scrutinize the way in which they have elaborated their consequences.

Now, to limit myself to existential philosophies, I see that all of them without exception suggest escape. Through an odd reasoning, starting out from the absurd over the ruins of reason, in a closed universe limited to the human, they deify what crushes them and find reason to hope in what impoverishes them. That forced hope is religious in all of them. It deserves attention.

I shall merely analyze here as examples a few themes dear to Chestov and Kierkegaard. But Jaspers will provide us, in caricatural form, a typical example of this attitude. As a result the rest will be clearer. He is left powerless to realize the transcendent, incapable of plumbing the depth of experience, and conscious of that universe upset by failure. Will he advance or at least draw the conclusions from that failure? He contributes nothing new. He has found nothing in experience but the confession of his own impotence and no occasion to infer any satisfactory principle. Yet without justification, as he says to himself, he suddenly asserts all at once the transcendent, the essence of experience, and the superhuman significance of life when he writes: "Does not the failure reveal, beyond any possible explanation and interpretation, not the absence but the existence of transcendence?" That existence which, suddenly and through a blind act of human confidence, explains everything, he defines as "the unthinkable unity of the general and the particular." Thus the absurd becomes god (in the broadest meaning of this word) and that inability to understand becomes the existence that illuminates everything. Nothing logically prepares this reasoning. I can call it a leap. And paradoxically can be understood Jaspers's insistence, his infinite patience devoted to making the experience of the transcendent impossible to realize. For the more fleeting that approximation is, the more empty that definition proves to be, and the more real that transcendent is to him; for the passion he devotes to asserting it is in direct proportion to the gap between his powers of explanation and the irrationality of the world and of experience. It thus appears that the more bitterly Jaspers destroys the reason's preconceptions, the more radically he will explain the world. That apostle of humiliated thought will find at the very end of humiliation the means of regenerating being to its very depth.

Mystical thought has familiarized us with such devices. They are just as legitimate as any attitude of mind. But for the moment I am acting as if I took a certain problem seriously. Without judging beforehand the general value of this attitude or its educative power, I mean simply to consider whether it answers the conditions I set myself, whether it is worthy of the conflict that concerns me. Thus I return to Chestov. A commentator relates a remark of his that deserves interest: "The only true solution," he said, "is precisely where human judgment sees no solution. Otherwise, what need would we have of God? We turn toward God only to obtain the impossible. As for the possible, men suffice." If there is a Chestovian philosophy, I can say that it is altogether summed up in this way. For when, at the conclusion of his passionate analyses, Chestov discovers the fundamental absurdity of all existence, he does not say: "This is the absurd," but rather: "This is God: we must rely on him even if he does not correspond to any of our rational categories." So that confusion may not be possible, the Russian philosopher even hints that this God is perhaps full of hatred and hateful, incomprehensible and contradictory; but the more hideous is his face, the more he asserts his power. His greatness is his incoherence. His proof is his inhumanity. One must spring into him and by this leap free oneself from rational illusions. Thus, for Chestov acceptance of the absurd is contemporaneous with the absurd itself. Being aware of it amounts to accepting it, and the whole logical effort of his thought is to bring it out so that at the same time the tremendous hope it involves may burst forth. Let me repeat that this attitude is legitimate. But I am persisting here in considering a single problem and all its consequences. I do not have to examine the emotion of a thought or of an act of faith. I have a whole lifetime to do that. I know that the rationalist finds Chestov's attitude annoying. But I also feel that Chestov is right rather than the rationalist, and I merely want to know if he remains faithful to the commandments of the absurd.

Now, if it is admitted that the absurd is the contrary of hope, it is seen that existential thought for Chestov presupposes the absurd but proves it only to dispel it. Such subtlety of thought is a conjuror's emotional trick. When Chestov elsewhere sets his absurd in opposition to current morality and reason, he calls it truth and redemption. Hence, there is basically in that definition of the absurd an approbation that Chestov grants it. If it is admitted that all the power of that notion lies in the way it runs counter to our elementary hopes, if it is felt that to remain, the absurd requires not to be consented to, then it can be clearly seen that it has lost its true aspect, its human and relative character in order to enter an eternity that is both incomprehensible and satisfying. If there is an absurd, it is in man's universe. The moment the notion transforms itself into eternity's springboard, it ceases to be linked to human lucidity. The absurd is no longer that evidence that man ascertains without consenting to it. The struggle is eluded. Man integrates the absurd and in that communion causes to disappear its essential character, which is opposition, laceration, and divorce. This leap is an escape. Chestov, who is so fond of quoting Hamlet's remark:

"The time is out of joint," writes it down with a sort of savage hope that seems to belong to him in particular. For it is not in this sense that Hamlet says it or Shakespeare writes it. The intoxication of the irrational and the vocation of rapture turn a lucid mind away from the absurd. To Chestov reason is useless but there is something beyond reason. To an absurd mind reason is useless and there is nothing beyond reason.

This leap can at least enlighten us a little more as to the true nature of the absurd. We know that it is worthless except in an equilibrium, that it is, above all, in the comparison and not in the terms of that comparison. But it so happens that Chestov puts all the emphasis on one of the terms and destroys the equilibrium. Our appetite for understanding, our nostalgia for the absolute are explicable only in so far, precisely, as we can understand and explain many things. It is useless to negate the reason absolutely. It has its order in which it is efficacious. It is properly that of human experience. Whence we wanted to make everything clear. If we cannot do so, if the absurd is born on that occasion, it is born precisely at the very meeting-point of that efficacious but limited reason with the ever resurgent irrational. Now, when Chestov rises up against a Hegelian proposition such as "the motion of the solar system takes place in conformity with immutable laws and those laws are its reason," when he devotes all his passion to upsetting Spinoza's rationalism, he concludes, in effect, in favor of the vanity of all reason. Whence, by a natural and illegitimate reversal, to the pre-eminence of the irrational.[5] But the transition is not evident. For here may intervene the notion of limit and the notion of level. The laws of nature may be operative up to a certain limit, beyond which they turn against themselves to give birth to the absurd. Or else, they may justify themselves on the level of description without for that reason being true on the level of explanation. Everything is sacrificed here to the irrational, and, the demand for clarity being conjured away, the absurd disappears with one of the terms of its comparison. The absurd man, on the other hand, does not undertake

[5] Apropos of the notion of exception particularly and against Aristotle.

such a leveling process. He recognizes the struggle, does not absolutely scorn reason, and admits the irrational. Thus he again embraces in a single glance all the data of experience and he is little inclined to leap before knowing. He knows simply that in that alert awareness there is no further place for hope.

What is perceptible in Leo Chestov will be perhaps even more so in Kierkegaard. To be sure, it is hard to outline clear propositions in so elusive a writer. But, despite apparently opposed writings, beyond the pseudonyms, the tricks, and the smiles, can be felt throughout that work, as it were, the presentiment (at the same time as the apprehension) of a truth which eventually bursts forth in the last works: Kierkegaard likewise takes the leap. His childhood having been so frightened by Christianity, he ultimately returns to its harshest aspect. For him, too, antinomy and paradox become criteria of the religious. Thus, the very thing that led to despair of the meaning and depth of this life now gives it its truth and its clarity. Christianity is the scandal, and what Kierkegaard calls for quite plainly is the third sacrifice required by Ignatius Loyola, the one in which God most rejoices: "The sacrifice of the intellect." [6] This effect of the "leap" is odd, but must not surprise us any longer. He makes of the absurd the criterion of the other world, whereas it is simply a residue of the experience of this world. "In his failure," says Kierkegaard, "the believer finds his triumph."

It is not for me to wonder to what stirring preaching this attitude is linked. I merely have to wonder if the spectacle of the absurd and its own character justifies it. On this point, I know that it is not so. Upon considering again the content of the absurd, one understands better the method that inspired Kierkegaard. Between the irrational of the world and the insurgent nostalgia of the absurd, he does not maintain the equilibrium. He does not respect the relationship that constitutes, properly

[6] It may be thought that I am neglecting here the essential problem, that of faith. But I am not examining the philosophy of Kierkegaard or of Chestov or, later on, of Husserl (this would call for a different place and a different attitude of mind); I am simply borrowing a theme from them and examining whether its consequences can fit the already established rules. It is merely a matter of persistence.

speaking, the feeling of absurdity. Sure of being unable to escape the irrational, he wants at least to save himself from that desperate nostalgia that seems to him sterile and devoid of implication. But if he may be right on this point in his judgment, he could not be in his negation. If he substitutes for his cry of revolt a frantic adherence, at once he is led to blind himself to the absurd which hitherto enlightened him and to deify the only certainty he henceforth possesses, the irrational. The important thing, as Abbé Galiani said to Mme d'Epinay, is not to be cured, but to live with one's ailments. Kierkegaard wants to be cured. To be cured is his frenzied wish, and it runs throughout his whole journal. The entire effort of his intelligence is to escape the antinomy of the human condition. An all the more desperate effort since he intermittently perceives its vanity when he speaks of himself, as if neither fear of God nor piety were capable of bringing him to peace. Thus it is that, through a strained subterfuge, he gives the irrational the appearance and God the attributes of the absurd: unjust, incoherent, and incomprehensible. Intelligence alone in him strives to stifle the underlying demands of the human heart. Since nothing is proved, everything can be proved.

Indeed, Kierkegaard himself shows us the path taken. I do not want to suggest anything here, but how can one fail to read in his works the signs of an almost intentional mutilation of the soul to balance the mutilation accepted in regard to the absurd? It is the leitmotiv of the *Journal.* "What I lacked was the animal which *also* belongs to human destiny. . . . But give me a body then." And further on: "Oh! especially in my early youth what should I not have given to be a man, even for six months . . . what I lack, basically, is a body and the physical conditions of existence." Elsewhere, the same man nevertheless adopts the great cry of hope that has come down through so many centuries and quickened so many hearts, except that of the absurd man. "But for the Christian death is certainly not the end of everything and it implies infinitely more hope than life implies for us, even when that life is overflowing with health and vigor." Reconciliation through scandal is still reconciliation. It allows one perhaps, as can be seen, to derive hope of its contrary, which is death. But even if fellow-feeling inclines one toward that attitude, still it must be said that excess justifies nothing. That transcends, as the saying goes, the human scale; therefore it must be superhuman. But this "therefore" is superfluous. There is no logical certainty here. There is no experimental probability either. All I can say is that, in fact, that transcends my scale. If I do not draw a negation from it, at least I do not want to found anything on the incomprehensible. I want to know whether I can live with what I know and with that alone. I am told again that here the intelligence must sacrifice its pride and the reason bow down. But if I recognize the limits of the reason, I do not therefore negate it, recognizing its relative powers. I merely want to remain in this middle path where the intelligence can remain clear. If that is its pride, I see no sufficient reason for giving it up. Nothing more profound, for example, than Kierkegaard's view according to which despair is not a fact but a state: the very state of sin. For sin is what alienates from God. The absurd, which is the metaphysical state of the conscious man, does not lead to God.[7] Perhaps this notion will become clearer if I risk this shocking statement: the absurd is sin without God.

It is a matter of living in that state of the absurd. I know on what it is founded, this mind and this world straining against each other without being able to embrace each other. I ask for the rule of life of that state, and what I am offered neglects its basis, negates one of the terms of the painful opposition, demands of me a resignation. I ask what is involved in the condition I recognize as mine; I know it implies obscurity and ignorance; and I am assured that this ignorance explains everything and that this darkness is my light. But there is no reply here to my intent, and this stirring lyricism cannot hide the paradox from me. One must therefore turn away. Kierkegaard may shout in warning: "If man had no eternal consciousness, if, at the bottom of everything, there were merely a wild, seething force producing everything, both large and trifling, in the storm of

[7] I did not say "excludes God," which would still amount to asserting.

dark passions, if the bottomless void that nothing can fill underlay all things, what would life be but despair?" This cry is not likely to stop the absurd man. Seeking what is true is not seeking what is desirable. If in order to elude the anxious question: "What would life be?" one must, like the donkey, feed on the roses of illusion, then the absurd mind, rather than resigning itself to falsehood, prefers to adopt fearlessly Kierkegaard's reply: "despair." Everything considered, a determined soul will always manage.

I am taking the liberty at this point of calling the existential attitude philosophical suicide. But this does not imply a judgment. It is a convenient way of indicating the movement by which a thought negates itself and tends to transcend itself in its very negation. For the existentials negation is their God. To be precise, that god is maintained only through the negation of human reason.[8] But, like suicides, gods change with men. There are many ways of leaping, the essential being to leap. Those redeeming negations, those ultimate contradictions which negate the obstacle that has not yet been leaped over, may spring just as well (this is the paradox at which this reasoning aims) from a certain religious inspiration as from the rational order. They always lay claim to the eternal, and it is solely in this that they take the leap.

It must be repeated that the reasoning developed in this essay leaves out altogether the most widespread spiritual attitude of our enlightened age: the one, based on the principle that all is reason, which aims to explain the world. It is natural to give a clear view of the world after accepting the idea that it must be clear. That is even legitimate, but does not concern the reasoning we are following out here. In fact, our aim is to shed light upon the step taken by the mind when, starting from a philosophy of the world's lack of meaning, it ends up by finding a meaning and depth in it. The most touch-

[8] Let me assert again: it is not the affirmation of God that is questioned here, but rather the logic leading to that affirmation.

ing of those steps is religious in essence; it becomes obvious in the theme of the irrational. But the most paradoxical and most significant is certainly the one that attributes rational reasons to a world it originally imagined as devoid of any guiding principle. It is impossible in any case to reach the consequences that concern us without having given an idea of this new attainment of the spirit of nostalgia.

I shall examine merely the theme of "the Intention" made fashionable by Husserl and the phenomenologists. I have already alluded to it. Originally Husserl's method negates the classic procedure of the reason. Let me repeat. Thinking is not unifying or making the appearance familiar under the guise of a great principle. Thinking is learning all over again how to see, directing one's consciousness, making of every image a privileged place. In other words, phenomenology declines to explain the world, it wants to be merely a description of actual experience. It confirms absurd thought in its initial assertion that there is no truth, but merely truths. From the evening breeze to this hand on my shoulder, everything has its truth. Consciousness illuminates it by paying attention to it. Consciousness does not form the object of its understanding, it merely focuses, it is the act of attention, and, to borrow a Bergsonian image, it resembles the projector that suddenly focuses on an image. The difference is that there is no scenario, but a successive and incoherent illustration. In that magic lantern all the pictures are privileged. Consciousness suspends in experience the objects of its attention. Through its miracle it isolates them. Henceforth they are beyond all judgments. This is the "intention" that characterizes consciousness. But the word does not imply any idea of finality; it is taken in its sense of "direction": its only value is topographical.

At first sight, it certainly seems that in this way nothing contradicts the absurd spirit. That apparent modesty of thought that limits itself to describing what it declines to explain, that intentional discipline whence result paradoxically a profound enrichment of experience and the rebirth of the world in its prolixity are absurd procedures. At least at first sight. For methods of thought, in this case as elsewhere, always assume two aspects, one psychological and the other metaphysical.[9] Thereby they harbor two truths. If the theme of the intentional claims to illustrate merely a psychological attitude, by which reality is drained instead of being explained, nothing in fact separates it from the absurd spirit. It aims to enumerate what it cannot transcend. It affirms solely that without any unifying principle thought can still take delight in describing and understanding every aspect of experience. The truth involved then for each of those aspects is psychological in nature. It simply testifies to the "interest" that reality can offer. It is a way of awaking a sleeping world and of making it vivid to the mind. But if one attempts to extend and give a rational basis to that notion of truth, if one claims to discover in this way the "essence" of each object of knowledge, one restores its depth to experience. For an absurd mind that is incomprehensible. Now, it is this wavering between modesty and assurance that is noticeable in the intentional attitude, and this shimmering of phenomenological thought will illustrate the absurd reasoning better than anything else.

For Husserl speaks likewise of "extra-temporal essences" brought to light by the intention, and he sounds like Plato. All things are not explained by one thing but by all things. I see no difference. To be sure, those ideas or those essences that consciousness "effectuates" at the end of every description are not yet to be considered perfect models. But it is asserted that they are directly present in each datum of perception. There is no longer a single idea explaining everything, but an infinite number of essences giving a meaning to an infinite number of objects. The world comes to a stop, but also lights up. Platonic realism becomes intuitive, but it is still realism. Kierkegaard was swallowed up in his God; Parmenides plunged thought into the One. But here thought hurls itself into an abstract polytheism. But this is not all: hallucinations and fictions likewise belong to "extra-temporal essences." In the new world of ideas, the species of centaurs collaborates with the more modest species of metropolitan man.

[9] Even the most rigorous epistemologies imply metaphysics. And to such a degree that the metaphysic of many contemporary thinkers consists in having nothing but an epistemology.

For the absurd man, there was a truth as well as a bitterness in that purely psychological opinion that all aspects of the world are privileged. To say that everything is privileged is tantamount to saying that everything is equivalent. But the metaphysical aspect of that truth is so far-reaching that through an elementary reaction he feels closer perhaps to Plato. He is taught, in fact, that every image presupposes an equally privileged essence. In this idea world without hierarchy, the formal army is composed solely of generals. To be sure, transcendency had been eliminated. But a sudden shift in thought brings back into the world a sort of fragmentary immanence which restores to the universe its depth.

Am I to fear having carried too far a theme handled with greater circumspection by its creators? I read merely these assertions of Husserl, apparently paradoxical yet rigorously logical if what precedes is accepted: "That which is true is true absolutely, in itself; truth is one, identical with itself, however different the creatures who perceive it, men, monsters, angels or gods." Reason triumphs and trumpets forth with that voice, I cannot deny. What can its assertions mean in the absurd world? The perception of an angel or a god has no meaning for me. That geometrical spot where divine reason ratifies mine will always be incomprehensible to me. There, too, I discern a leap, and though performed in the abstract, it nonetheless means for me forgetting just what I do not want to forget. When farther on Husserl exclaims: "If all masses subject to attraction were to disappear, the law of attraction would not be destroyed but would simply remain without any possible application," I know that I am faced with a metaphysic of consolation. And if I want to discover the point where thought leaves the path of evidence, I have only to reread the parallel reasoning that Husserl voices regarding the mind: "If we could contemplate clearly the exact laws of psychic processes, they would be seen to be likewise eternal and invariable, like the basic laws of theoretical natural science. Hence they would be valid even if there were no psychic process." Even if the mind were not, its laws would be! I see then that of a psychological truth Husserl aims to make a rational rule: after having denied the integrating power of human reason, he leaps by this expedient to eternal Reason.

Husserl's theme of the "concrete universe" cannot then surprise me. If I am told that all essences are not formal but that some are material, that the first are the object of logic and the second of science, this is merely a question of definition. The abstract, I am told, indicates but a part, without consistency in itself, of a concrete universal. But the wavering already noted allows me to throw light on the confusion of these terms. For that may mean that the concrete object of my attention, this sky, the reflection of that water on this coat, alone preserve the prestige of the real that my interest isolates in the world. And I shall not deny it. But that may mean also that this coat itself is universal, has its particular and sufficient essence, belongs to the world of forms. I then realize that merely the order of the procession has been changed. This world has ceased to have its reflection in a higher universe, but the heaven of forms is figured in the host of images of this earth. This changes nothing for me. Rather than encountering here a taste for the concrete, the meaning of the human condition, I find an intellectualism sufficiently unbridled to generalize the concrete itself.

It is futile to be amazed by the apparent paradox that leads thought to its own negation by the opposite paths of humiliated reason and triumphal reason. From the abstract god of Husserl to the dazzling god of Kierkegaard the distance is not so great. Reason and the irrational lead to the same preaching. In truth the way matters but little; the will to arrive suffices. The abstract philosopher and the religious philosopher start out from the same disorder and support each other in the same anxiety. But the essential is to explain. Nostalgia is stronger here than knowledge. It is significant that the thought of the epoch is at once one of the most deeply imbued with a philosophy of the non-significance of the world and one of the most divided in its conclusions. It is constantly oscillating between extreme rationalization of reality which tends to break up that thought into standard reasons and its extreme irrationalization which tends to deify it. But this divorce is only apparent. It is a matter of reconciliation, and, in both cases, the leap suffices. It is always wrongly thought that the notion of reason is a one-way notion. To tell the truth, however rigorous it may be in its ambition, this concept is nonetheless just as unstable as others. Reason bears a quite human aspect, but it also is able to turn toward the divine. Since Plotinus, who was the first to reconcile it with the eternal climate, it has learned to turn away from the most cherished of its principles, which is contradiction, in order to integrate into it the strangest, the quite magic one of participation.[1] It is an instrument of thought and not thought itself. Above all, a man's thought is his nostalgia.

Just as reason was able to soothe the melancholy of Plotinus, it provides modern anguish the means of calming itself in the familiar setting of the eternal. The absurd mind has less luck. For it the world is neither so rational nor so irrational. It is unreasonable and only that. With Husserl the reason eventually has no limits at all. The absurd, on the contrary, establishes its limits since it is powerless to calm its anguish. Kierkegaard independently asserts that a single limit is enough to negate that anguish. But the absurd does not go so far. For it that limit is directed solely at the reason's ambitions. The theme of the irrational, as it is conceived by the existentials, is reason becoming confused and escaping by negating itself. The absurd is lucid reason noting its limits.

Only at the end of this difficult path does the absurd man recognize his true motives. Upon comparing his inner exigence and what is then offered him, he suddenly feels he is going to turn away. In the universe of Husserl the world becomes clear and that longing for familiarity that man's heart harbors becomes useless. In Kierkegaard's apocalypse that desire for clarity must be given up if it wants to be satisfied. Sin is not so much knowing (if it

---

[1] A.—At that time reason had to adapt itself or die. It adapts itself. With Plotinus, after being logical it becomes æsthetic. Metaphor takes the place of the syllogism.

B.—Moreover, this is not Plotinus' only contribution to phenomenology. This whole attitude is already contained in the concept so dear to the Alexandrian thinker that there is not only an idea of man but also an idea of Socrates.

were, everybody would be innocent) as wanting to know. Indeed, it is the only sin of which the absurd man can feel that it constitutes both his guilt and his innocence. He is offered a solution in which all the past contradictions have become merely polemical games. But this is not the way he experienced them. Their truth must be preserved, which consists in not being satisfied. He does not want preaching.

My reasoning wants to be faithful to the evidence that aroused it. That evidence is the absurd. It is that divorce between the mind that desires and the world that disappoints, my nostalgia for unity, this fragmented universe and the contradiction that binds them together. Kierkegaard suppresses my nostalgia and Husserl gathers together that universe. That is not what I was expecting. It was a matter of living and thinking with those dislocations, of knowing whether one had to accept or refuse. There can be no question of masking the evidence, of suppressing the absurd by denying one of the terms of its equation. It is essential to know whether one can live with it or whether, on the other hand, logic commands one to die of it. I am not interested in philosophical suicide, but rather in plain suicide. I merely wish to purge it of its emotional content and know its logic and its integrity. Any other position implies for the absurd mind deceit and the mind's retreat before what the mind itself has brought to light. Husserl claims to obey the desire to escape "the inveterate habit of living and thinking in certain well-known and convenient conditions of existence," but the final leap restores in him the eternal and its comfort. The leap does not represent an extreme danger as Kierkegaard would like it to do. The danger, on the contrary, lies in the subtle instant that precedes the leap. Being able to remain on that dizzying crest—that is integrity and the rest is subterfuge. I know also that never has helplessness inspired such striking harmonies as those of Kierkegaard. But if helplessness has its place in the indifferent landscapes of history, it has none in a reasoning whose exigence is now known.

Absurd Freedom

Now the main thing is done, I hold certain facts from which I cannot separate. What I know, what is certain, what I cannot deny, what I cannot reject—this is what counts. I can negate everything of that part of me that lives on vague nostalgias, except this desire for unity, this longing to solve, this need for clarity and cohesion. I can refute everything in this world surrounding me that offends or enraptures me, except this chaos, this sovereign chance and this divine equivalence which springs from anarchy. I don't know whether this world has a meaning that transcends it. But I know that I do not know that meaning and that it is impossible for me just now to know it. What can a meaning outside my condition mean to me? I can understand only in human terms. What I touch, what resists me—that is what I understand. And these two certainties—my appetite for the absolute and for unity and the impossibility of reducing this world to a rational and reasonable principle—I also know that I cannot reconcile them. What other truth can I admit without lying, without bringing in a hope I lack and which means nothing within the limits of my condition?

If I were a tree among trees, a cat among animals, this life would have a meaning, or rather this problem would not arise, for I should belong to this world. I should *be* this world to which I am now opposed by my whole consciousness and my whole insistence upon familiarity. This ridiculous reason is what sets me in opposition to all creation. I cannot cross it out with a stroke of the pen. What I believe to be true I must therefore preserve. What seems to me so obvious, even against me, I must support. And what constitutes the basis of that conflict, of that break between the world and my mind, but the awareness of it? If therefore I want to preserve it, I can through a constant awareness, ever revived, ever alert. This is what, for the moment, I must remember. At this moment the absurd, so obvious and yet so hard to win, returns to a man's life and finds its home there. At this moment, too, the mind can leave the arid, dried-up path of lucid effort. That path now emerges in daily life. It encounters the world of the anonymous impersonal pronoun "one," but henceforth man enters in with his revolt and his lucidity. He has forgotten how to hope. This hell of the present is his Kingdom at last. All problems recover their sharp edge. Abstract evidence retreats before the poetry of forms and colors. Spiritual conflicts become embodied and return to the abject and magnificent shelter of man's heart. None of them is settled. But all are transfigured. Is one going to die, escape by the leap, rebuild a mansion of ideas and forms to one's own scale? Is one, on the contrary, going to take up the heart-rending and marvelous wager of the absurd? Let's make a final effort in this regard and draw all our conclusions. The body, affection, creation, action, human nobility will then resume their places in this mad world. At last man will again find there the wine of the absurd and the bread of indifference on which he feeds his greatness.

Let us insist again on the method: it is a matter of persisting. At a certain point on his path the absurd man is tempted. History is not lacking in either religions or prophets, even without gods. He is asked to leap. All he can reply is that he doesn't fully understand, that it is not obvious. Indeed, he does not want to do anything but what he fully understands. He is assured that this is the sin of pride, but he does not understand the notion of sin; that perhaps hell is in store, but he has not enough imagination to visualize that strange future; that he is losing immortal life, but that seems to him an idle consideration. An attempt is made to get him to admit his guilt. He feels innocent. To tell the truth, that is all he feels—his irreparable innocence. This is what allows him everything. Hence, what he demands of himself is to live *solely* with what he knows, to accommodate himself to what is, and to bring in nothing that is not certain. He is told that nothing is. But this at least is a certainty. And it is with this that he is concerned: he wants to find out if it is possible to live *without appeal*.

Now I can broach the notion of suicide. It has already been felt what solution might be given. At this point the problem is reversed. It was previously a question of finding out whether or not life had to have a meaning to be lived. It now becomes clear, on the contrary, that it will be lived all the better if it has no meaning. Living an experience, a particular fate, is accepting it fully. Now, no one will live this fate, knowing it to be absurd, unless he does everything to keep before him that absurd brought to light by consciousness. Negating one of the terms of the opposition on which he lives amounts to escaping it. To abolish conscious revolt is to elude the problem. The theme of permanent revolution is thus carried into individual experience. Living is keeping the absurd alive. Keeping it alive is, above all, contemplating it. Unlike Eurydice, the absurd dies only when we turn away from it. One of the only coherent philosophical positions is thus revolt. It is a constant confrontation between man and his own obscurity. It is an insistence upon an impossible transparency. It challenges the world anew every second. Just as danger provided man the unique opportunity of seizing awareness, so metaphysical revolt extends awareness to the whole of experience. It is that constant presence of man in his own eyes. It is not aspiration, for it is devoid of hope. That revolt is the certainty of a crushing fate, without the resignation that ought to accompany it.

This is where it is seen to what a degree absurd experience is remote from suicide. It may be thought that suicide follows revolt—but wrongly. For it does not represent the logical outcome of revolt. It is just the contrary by the consent it presupposes. Suicide, like the leap, is acceptance at its extreme. Everything is over and man returns to his essential history. His future, his unique and dreadful future—he sees and rushes toward it. In its way, suicide settles the absurd. It engulfs the absurd in the same death. But I know that in order to keep alive, the absurd cannot be settled. It escapes suicide to the extent that it is simultaneously awareness and rejection of death. It is, at the extreme limit of the condemned man's last thought, that shoelace that despite everything he sees a few yards away, on the very brink of his dizzying fall. The contrary of suicide, in fact, is the man condemned to death.

That revolt gives life its value. Spread out over the whole length of a life, it restores its majesty to that life.

To a man devoid of blinders, there is no finer sight than that of the intelligence at grips with a reality that transcends it. The sight of human pride is unequaled. No disparagement is of any use. That discipline that the mind imposes on itself, that will conjured up out of nothing, that face-to-face struggle have something exceptional about them. To impoverish that reality whose inhumanity constitutes man's majesty is tantamount to impoverishing him himself. I understand then why the doctrines that explain everything to me also debilitate me at the same time. They relieve me of the weight of my own life, and yet I must carry it alone. At this juncture, I cannot conceive that a skeptical metaphysics can be joined to an ethics of renunciation.

Consciousness and revolt, these rejections are the contrary of renunciation. Everything that is indomitable and passionate in a human heart quickens them, on the contrary, with its own life. It is essential to die unreconciled and not of one's own free will. Suicide is a repudiation. The absurd man can only drain everything to the bitter end, and deplete himself. The absurd is his extreme tension, which he maintains constantly by solitary effort, for he knows that in that consciousness and in that day-to-day revolt he gives proof of his only truth, which is defiance. This is a first consequence.

If I remain in that prearranged position which consists in drawing all the conclusions (and nothing else) involved in a newly discovered notion, I am faced with a second paradox. In order to remain faithful to that method, I have nothing to do with the problem of metaphysical liberty. Knowing whether or not man is free doesn't interest me. I can experience only my own freedom. As to it, I can have no general notions, but merely a few clear insights. The problem of "freedom as such" has no meaning. For it is linked in quite a different way with the problem of God. Knowing whether or not man is free involves knowing whether he can have a master. The absurdity peculiar to this problem comes from the fact that the very notion that makes the problem of freedom possible also takes away all its meaning. For in the presence of God there is less a problem of freedom than a problem of evil. You know the alternative: either we are not free and God the all-powerful is responsible for evil. Or we are free and responsible but God is not all-powerful. All the scholastic subtleties have neither added anything to nor subtracted anything from the acuteness of this paradox.

This is why I cannot get lost in the glorification or the mere definition of a notion which eludes me and loses its meaning as soon as it goes beyond the frame of reference of my individual experience. I cannot understand what kind of freedom would be given me by a higher being. I have lost the sense of hierarchy. The only conception of freedom I can have is that of the prisoner or the individual in the midst of the State. The only one I know is freedom of thought and action. Now if the absurd cancels all my chances of eternal freedom, it restores and magnifies, on the other hand, my freedom of action. That privation of hope and future means an increase in man's availability.

Before encountering the absurd, the everyday man lives with aims, a concern for the future or for justification (with regard to whom or what is not the question). He weighs his chances, he counts on "someday," his retirement or the labor of his sons. He still thinks that something in his life can be directed. In truth, he acts as if he were free, even if all the facts make a point of contradicting that liberty. But after the absurd, everything is upset. That idea that "I am," my way of acting as if everything has a meaning (even if, on occasion, I said that nothing has)—all that is given the lie in vertiginous fashion by the absurdity of a possible death. Thinking of the future, establishing aims for oneself, having preferences—all this presupposes a belief in freedom, even if one occasionally ascertains that one doesn't feel it. But at that moment I am well aware that that higher liberty, that freedom *to be*, which alone can serve as basis for a truth, does not exist. Death is there as the only reality. After death the chips are down. I am not even free, either, to perpetuate myself, but a slave, and, above all, a slave without hope of an eternal revolution, without recourse to contempt. And who without revolution and without contempt can remain a slave? What freedom can exist in the fullest sense without assurance of eternity?

But at the same time the absurd man realizes that hitherto he was bound to that postulate of freedom on the illusion of which he was living. In a certain sense, that hampered him. To the extent to which he imagined a purpose to his life, he adapted himself to the demands of a purpose to be achieved and became the slave of his liberty. Thus I could not act otherwise than as the father (or the engineer or the leader of a nation, or the post-office sub-clerk) that I am preparing to be. I think I can choose to be that rather than something else. I think so unconsciously, to be sure. But at the same time I strengthen my postulate with the beliefs of those around me, with the presumptions of my human environment (others are so sure of being free, and that cheerful mood is so contagious!). However far one may remain from any presumption, moral or social, one is partly influenced by them and even, for the best among them (there are good and bad presumptions), one adapts one's life to them. Thus the absurd man realizes that he was not really free. To speak clearly, to the extent to which I hope, to which I worry about a truth that might be individual to me, about a way of being or creating, to the extent to which I arrange my life and prove thereby that I accept its having a meaning, I create for myself barriers between which I confine my life. I do like so many bureaucrats of the mind and heart who only fill me with disgust and whose only vice, I now see clearly, is to take man's freedom seriously.

The absurd enlightens me on this point: there is no future. Henceforth this is the reason for my inner freedom. I shall use two comparisons here. Mystics, to begin with, find freedom in giving themselves. By losing themselves in their god, by accepting his rules, they become secretly free. In spontaneously accepted slavery they recover a deeper independence. But what does that freedom mean? It may be said, above all, that they *feel* free with regard to themselves, and not so much free as liberated. Likewise, completely turned toward death (taken here as the most obvious absurdity), the absurd man feels released from everything outside that passionate attention crystallizing in him. He enjoys a freedom with regard to common rules. It can be seen at this point that the initial themes of existential philosophy keep their entire value. The return to consciousness, the escape from everyday sleep represent the first steps of absurd freedom. But it is existential *preaching* that is alluded to, and with it that spiritual leap which basically escapes consciousness. In the same way (this is my second comparison) the slaves of antiquity did not belong to themselves. But they knew that freedom which consists in not feeling responsible.[2] Death, too, has patrician hands which, while crushing, also liberate.

Losing oneself in that bottomless certainty, feeling henceforth sufficiently remote from one's own life to increase it and take a broad view of it—this involves the principle of a liberation. Such new independence has a definite time limit, like any freedom of action. It does not write a check on eternity. But it takes the place of the illusions of *freedom*, which all stopped with death. The divine availability of the condemned man before whom the prison doors open in a certain early dawn, that unbelievable disinterestedness with regard to everything except for the pure flame of life—it is clear that death and the absurd are here the principles of the only reasonable freedom: that which a human heart can experience and live. This is a second consequence. The absurd man thus catches sight of a burning and frigid, transparent and limited universe in which nothing is possible but everything is given, and beyond which all is collapse and nothingness. He can then decide to accept such a universe and draw from it his strength, his refusal to hope, and the unyielding evidence of a life without consolation.

But what does life mean in such a universe? Nothing else for the moment but indifference to the future and a desire to use up everything that is given. Belief in the

[2] I am concerned here with a factual comparison, not with an apology of humility. The absurd man is the contrary of the reconciled man.

meaning of life always implies a scale of values, a choice, our preferences. Belief in the absurd, according to our definitions, teaches the contrary. But this is worth examining.

Knowing whether or not one can live *without appeal* is all that interests me. I do not want to get out of my depth. This aspect of life being given me, can I adapt myself to it? Now, faced with this particular concern, belief in the absurd is tantamount to substituting the quantity of experiences for the quality. If I convince myself that this life has no other aspect than that of the absurd, if I feel that its whole equilibrium depends on that perpetual opposition between my conscious revolt and the darkness in which it struggles, if I admit that my freedom has no meaning except in relation to its limited fate, then I must say that what counts is not the best living but the most living. It is not up to me to wonder if this is vulgar or revolting, elegant or deplorable. Once and for all, value judgments are discarded here in favor of factual judgments. I have merely to draw the conclusions from what I can see and to risk nothing that is hypothetical. Supposing that living in this way were not honorable, then true propriety would command me to be dishonorable.

The most living; in the broadest sense, that rule means nothing. It calls for definition. It seems to begin with the fact that the notion of quantity has not been sufficiently explored. For it can account for a large share of human experience. A man's rule of conduct and his scale of values have no meaning except through the quantity and variety of experiences he has been in a position to accumulate. Now, the conditions of modern life impose on the majority of men the same quantity of experiences and consequently the same profound experience. To be sure, there must also be taken into consideration the individual's spontaneous contribution, the "given" element in him. But I cannot judge of that, and let me repeat that my rule here is to get along with the immediate evidence. I see, then, that the individual character of a common code of ethics lies not so much in the ideal importance of its basic principles as in the norm of an experience that it is possible to measure. To stretch a point somewhat, the Greeks had the code of their leisure just as we have the code of our eight-hour day. But already many men among the most tragic cause us to foresee that a longer experience changes this table of values. They make us imagine that adventurer of the everyday who through mere quantity of experiences would break all records (I am purposely using this sports expression) and would thus win his own code of ethics.[3] Yet let's avoid romanticism and just ask ourselves what such an attitude may mean to a man with his mind made up to take up his bet and to observe strictly what he takes to be the rules of the game.

Breaking all the records is first and foremost being faced with the world as often as possible. How can that be done without contradictions and without playing on words? For on the one hand the absurd teaches that all experiences are unimportant, and on the other it urges toward the greatest quantity of experiences. How, then, can one fail to do as so many of those men I was speaking of earlier—choose the form of life that brings us the most possible of that human matter, thereby introducing a scale of values that on the other hand one claims to reject?

But again it is the absurd and its contradictory life that teaches us. For the mistake is thinking that that quantity of experiences depends on the circumstances of our life when it depends solely on us. Here we have to be over-simple. To two men living the same number of years, the world always provides the same sum of experiences. It is up to us to be conscious of them. Being aware of one's life, one's revolt, one's freedom, and to the maximum, is living, and to the maximum. Where lucidity dominates, the scale of values becomes useless. Let's be even more simple. Let us say that the sole obstacle, the sole deficiency to be made good, is constituted by premature death. Thus it is that no depth, no emotion, no passion, and no sacrifice could render equal in the eyes of the absurd man (even if he wished it so) a conscious life of forty years and a lucidity spread over

[3] Quantity sometimes constitutes quality. If I can believe the latest restatements of scientific theory, all matter is constituted by centers of energy. Their greater or lesser quantity makes its specificity more or

sixty years.[4] Madness and death are his irreparables. Man does not choose. The absurd and the extra life it involves *therefore do not depend on man's will,* but on its contrary, which is death.[5] Weighing words carefully, it is altogether a question of luck. One just has to be able to consent to this. There will never be any substitute for twenty years of life and experience.

By what is an odd inconsistency in such an alert race, the Greeks claimed that those who died young were beloved of the gods. And that is true only if you are willing to believe that entering the ridiculous world of the gods is forever losing the purest of joys, which is feeling, and feeling on this earth. The present and the succession of presents before a constantly conscious soul is the ideal of the absurd man. But the word "ideal" rings false in this connection. It is not even his vocation, but merely the third consequence of his reasoning. Having started from an anguished awareness of the inhuman, the meditation on the absurd returns at the end of its itinerary to the very heart of the passionate flames of human revolt.[6]

Thus I draw from the absurd three consequences, which are my revolt, my freedom, and my passion. By the mere activity of consciousness I transform into a rule of life what was an invitation to death—and I refuse suicide. I know, to be sure, the dull resonance that vibrates throughout these days. Yet I have but a word to

less remarkable. A billion ions and one ion differ not only in quantity but also in quality. It is easy to find an analogy in human experience.

[4] Same reflection on a notion as different as the idea of eternal nothingness. It neither adds anything to nor subtracts anything from reality. In psychological experience of nothingness, it is by the consideration of what will happen in two thousand years that our own nothingness truly takes on meaning. In one of its aspects, eternal nothingness is made up precisely of the sum of lives to come which will not be ours.

[5] The will is only the agent here: it tends to maintain consciousness. It provides a discipline of life, and that is appreciable.

[6] What matters is coherence. We start out here from acceptance of the world. But Oriental thought teaches that one can indulge in the same effort of logic by choosing *against* the world. That is just as legitimate and gives this essay its perspectives and its limits. But when the negation of the world is pursued just as rigorously, one often achieves (in certain Vedantic schools) similar results regarding, for instance, the indifference of works. In a book of great importance, *Le Choix,* Jean Grenier establishes in this way a veritable "philosophy of indifference."

say: that it is necessary. When Nietzsche writes: "It clearly seems that the chief thing in heaven and on earth is to *obey* at length and in a single direction: in the long run there results something for which it is worth the trouble of living on this earth as, for example, virtue, art, music, the dance, reason, the mind—something that transfigures, something delicate, mad, or divine," he elucidates the rule of a really distinguished code of ethics. But he also points the way of the absurd man. Obeying the flame is both the easiest and the hardest thing to do. However, it is good for man to judge himself occasionally. He is alone in being able to do so.

"Prayer," says Alain, "is when night descends over thought." "But the mind must meet the night," reply the mystics and the existentials. Yes, indeed, but not that night that is born under closed eyelids and through the mere will of man—dark, impenetrable night that the mind calls up in order to plunge into it. If it must encounter a night, let it be rather that of despair, which remains lucid—polar night, vigil of the mind, whence will arise perhaps that white and virginal brightness which outlines every object in the light of the intelligence. At that degree, equivalence encounters passionate understanding. Then it is no longer even a question of judging the existential leap. It resumes its place amid the age-old fresco of human attitudes. For the spectator, if he is conscious, that leap is still absurd. In so far as it thinks it solves the paradox, it reinstates it intact. On this score, it is stirring. On this score, everything resumes its place and the absurd world is reborn in all its splendor and diversity.

But it is bad to stop, hard to be satisfied with a single way of seeing, to go without contradiction, perhaps the most subtle of all spiritual forces. The preceding merely defines a way of thinking. But the point is to live.

The Absurd Man

*If Stavrogin believes, he does not think he believes.
If he does not believe, he does not think he does
not believe.*

THE POSSESSED

"My field," said Goethe, "is time." That is indeed
the absurd speech. What, in fact, is the absurd man? He
who, without negating it, does nothing for the eternal.
Not that nostalgia is foreign to him. But he prefers his
courage and his reasoning. The first teaches him to live
without appeal and to get along with what he has; the
second informs him of his limits. Assured of his temporally
limited freedom, of his revolt devoid of future, and of his
mortal consciousness, he lives out his adventure within
the span of his lifetime. That is his field, that is his action,
which he shields from any judgment but his own. A greater
life cannot mean for him another life. That would be un-
fair. I am not even speaking here of that paltry eternity
that is called posterity. Mme Roland relied on herself.
That rashness was taught a lesson. Posterity is glad to quote
her remark, but forgets to judge it. Mme Roland is indifferent to posterity.

There can be no question of holding forth on ethics.
I have seen people behave badly with great morality and
I note every day that integrity has no need of rules.
There is but one moral code that the absurd man can
accept, the one that is not separated from God: the one
that is dictated. But it so happens that he lives outside
that God. As for the others (I mean also immoralism),

the absurd man sees nothing in them but justifications and he has nothing to justify. I start out here from the principle of his innocence.

That innocence is to be feared. "Everything is permitted," exclaims Ivan Karamazov. That, too, smacks of the absurd. But on condition that it not be taken in the vulgar sense. I don't know whether or not it has been sufficiently pointed out that it is not an outburst of relief or of joy, but rather a bitter acknowledgment of a fact. The certainty of a God giving a meaning to life far surpasses in attractiveness the ability to behave badly with impunity. The choice would not be hard to make. But there is no choice, and that is where the bitterness comes in. The absurd does not liberate; it binds. It does not authorize all actions. "Everything is permitted" does not mean that nothing is forbidden. The absurd merely confers an equivalence on the consequences of those actions. It does not recommend crime, for this would be childish, but it restores to remorse its futility. Likewise, if all experiences are indifferent, that of duty is as legitimate as any other. One can be virtuous through a whim.

All systems of morality are based on the idea that an action has consequences that legitimize or cancel it. A mind imbued with the absurd merely judges that those consequences must be considered calmly. It is ready to pay up. In other words, there may be responsible persons, but there are no guilty ones, in its opinion. At very most, such a mind will consent to use past experience as a basis for its future actions. Time will prolong time, and life will serve life. In this field that is both limited and bulging with possibilities, everything in himself, except his lucidity, seems unforeseeable to him. What rule, then, could emanate from that unreasonable order? The only truth that might seem instructive to him is not formal: it comes to life and unfolds in men. The absurd mind cannot so much expect ethical rules at the end of its reasoning as, rather, illustrations and the breath of human lives. The few following images are of this type. They prolong the absurd reasoning by giving it a specific attitude and their warmth.

Do I need to develop the idea that an example is not

necessarily an example to be followed (even less so, if possible, in the absurd world) and that these illustrations are not therefore models? Besides the fact that a certain vocation is required for this, one becomes ridiculous, with all due allowance, when drawing from Rousseau the conclusion that one must walk on all fours and from Nietzsche that one must maltreat one's mother. "It is essential to be absurd," writes a modern author, "it is not essential to be a dupe." The attitudes of which I shall treat can assume their whole meaning only through consideration of their contraries. A sub-clerk in the post office is the equal of a conqueror if consciousness is common to them. All experiences are indifferent in this regard. There are some that do either a service or a disservice to man. They do him a service if he is conscious. Otherwise, that has no importance: a man's failures imply judgment, not of circumstances, but of himself.

I am choosing solely men who aim only to expend themselves or whom I see to be expending themselves. That has no further implications. For the moment I want to speak only of a world in which thoughts, like lives, are devoid of future. Everything that makes man work and get excited utilizes hope. The sole thought that is not mendacious is therefore a sterile thought. In the absurd world the value of a notion or of a life is measured by its sterility.

Don Juanism

If it were sufficient to love, things would be too easy. The more one loves, the stronger the absurd grows. It is not through lack of love that Don Juan goes from woman to woman. It is ridiculous to represent him as a mystic in quest of total love. But it is indeed because he loves them with the same passion and each time with his whole self that he must repeat his gift and his profound quest. Whence each woman hopes to give him what no one has ever given him. Each time they are utterly wrong and merely manage to make him feel the need of that repetition. "At last," exclaims one of them, "I have given you love." Can we be surprised that Don Juan laughs at this? "At last? No," he says, "but once more." Why should it be essential to love rarely in order to love much?

Is Don Juan melancholy? This is not likely. I shall barely have recourse to the legend. That laugh, the conquering insolence, that playfulness and love of the theater are all clear and joyous. Every healthy creature tends to multiply himself. So it is with Don Juan. But, furthermore, melancholy people have two reasons for being so: they don't know or they hope. Don Juan knows and does not hope. He reminds one of those artists who know their limits, never go beyond them, and in that precarious interval in which they take their spiritual stand enjoy all the wonderful ease of masters. And that is indeed genius: the intelligence that knows its frontiers. Up to the frontier of physical death Don Juan is ignorant of melancholy. The moment he knows, his laugh bursts forth and makes one forgive everything. He was melancholy at the time when he hoped. Today, on the mouth of that woman he recognizes the bitter and comforting taste of the only knowledge. Bitter? Barely: that necessary imperfection that makes happiness perceptible!

It is quite false to try to see in Don Juan a man brought up on Ecclesiastes. For nothing is vanity to him except the hope of another life. He proves this because he gambles that other life against heaven itself. Longing for desire killed by satisfaction, that commonplace of the impotent man, does not belong to him. That is all right for Faust, who believed in God enough to sell himself to the devil. For Don Juan the thing is simpler. Molina's *Burlador* ever replies to the threats of hell: "What a long respite you give me!" What comes after death is futile, and what a long succession of days for whoever knows how to be alive! Faust craved worldly goods; the poor man had only to stretch out his hand. It already amounted to selling his soul when he was unable to gladden it. As for satiety, Don Juan insists upon it, on the contrary. If he leaves a woman it is not absolutely because he has ceased to desire her. A beautiful woman is always desirable. But he desires another, and no, this is not the same thing.

This life gratifies his every wish, and nothing is worse than losing it. This madman is a great wise man. But men who live on hope do not thrive in this universe where kindness yields to generosity, affection to virile silence, and communion to solitary courage. And all hasten to say: "He was a weakling, an idealist or a saint." One has to disparage the greatness that insults.

People are sufficiently annoyed (or that smile of complicity that debases what it admires) by Don Juan's speeches and by that same remark that he uses on all women. But to anyone who seeks quantity in his joys, the only thing that matters is efficacy. What is the use of complicating the passwords that have stood the test? No one, neither the woman nor the man, listens to them, but rather to the voice that pronounces them. They are the rule, the convention, and the courtesy. After they are spoken the most important still remains to be done. Don Juan is already getting ready for it. Why should he give himself a problem in morality? He is not like Milosz's Mañara, who damns himself through a desire to be a saint. Hell for him is a thing to be provoked. He has but one reply to divine wrath, and that is human honor: "I have honor," he says to the Commander, "and I am keeping my promise because I am a knight." But it would be just as great an error to make an immoralist of him. In this regard, he is "like everyone else": he has the moral code of his likes and dislikes. Don Juan can be properly understood only by constant reference to what he commonly symbolizes: the ordinary seducer and the sexual athlete. He *is* an ordinary seducer.[1] Except for the difference that he is conscious, and that is why he is absurd. A seducer who has become lucid will not change for all that. Seducing is his condition in life. Only in novels does one change condition or become better. Yet it can be said that at the same time nothing

[1] In the fullest sense and with his faults. A healthy attitude *also* includes faults.

is changed and everything is transformed. What Don Juan realizes in action is an ethic of quantity, whereas the saint, on the contrary, tends toward quality. Not to believe in the profound meaning of things belongs to the absurd man. As for those cordial or wonder-struck faces, he eyes them, stores them up, and does not pause over them. Time keeps up with him. The absurd man is he who is not apart from time. Don Juan does not think of "collecting" women. He exhausts their number and with them his chances of life. "Collecting" amounts to being capable of living off one's past. But he rejects regret, that other form of hope. He is incapable of looking at portraits.

Is he selfish for all that? In his way, probably. But here, too, it is essential to understand one another. There are those who are made for living and those who are made for loving. At least Don Juan would be inclined to say so. But he would do so in a very few words such as he is capable of choosing. For the love we are speaking of here is clothed in illusions of the eternal. As all the specialists in passion teach us, there is no eternal love but what is thwarted. There is scarcely any passion without struggle. Such a love culminates only in the ultimate contradiction of death. One must be Werther or nothing. There, too, there are several ways of committing suicide, one of which is the total gift and forgetfulness of self. Don Juan, as well as anyone else, knows that this can be stirring. But he is one of the very few who know that this is not the important thing. He knows just as well that those who turn away from all personal life through a great love enrich themselves perhaps but certainly impoverish those their love has chosen. A mother or a passionate wife necessarily has a closed heart, for it is turned away from the world. A single emotion, a single creature, a single face, but all is devoured. Quite a different love disturbs Don Juan, and this one is liberating. It brings with it all the faces in the world, and its tremor comes from the fact that it knows itself to be mortal. Don Juan has chosen to be nothing.

For him it is a matter of seeing clearly. We call love

what binds us to certain creatures only by reference to a collective way of seeing for which books and legends are responsible. But of love I know only that mixture of desire, affection, and intelligence that binds me to this or that creature. That compound is not the same for another person. I do not have the right to cover all these experiences with the same name. This exempts one from conducting them with the same gestures. The absurd man multiplies here again what he cannot unify. Thus he discovers a new way of being which liberates him at least as much as it liberates those who approach him. There is no noble love but that which recognizes itself to be both short-lived and exceptional. All those deaths and all those rebirths gathered together as in a sheaf make up for Don Juan the flowering of his life. It is his way of giving and of vivifying. I let it be decided whether or not one can speak of selfishness.

I think at this point of all those who absolutely insist that Don Juan be punished. Not only in another life, but even in this one. I think of all those tales, legends, and laughs about the aged Don Juan. But Don Juan is already ready. To a conscious man old age and what it portends are not a surprise. Indeed, he is conscious only in so far as he does not conceal its horror from himself. There was in Athens a temple dedicated to old age. Children were taken there. As for Don Juan, the more people laugh at him, the more his figure stands out. Thereby he rejects the one the romantics lent him. No one wants to laugh at that tormented, pitiful Don Juan. He is pitied; heaven itself will redeem him? But that's not it. In the universe of which Don Juan has a glimpse, ridicule *too* is included. He would consider it normal to be chastised. That is the rule of the game. And, indeed, it is typical of his nobility to have accepted all the rules of the game. Yet he knows he is right and that there can be no question of punishment. A fate is not a punishment.

That is his crime, and how easy it is to understand why the men of God call down punishment on his head. He achieves a knowledge without illusions which negates everything they profess. Loving and possessing, conquering and consuming—that is his way of knowing. (There is significance in that favorite Scriptural word that calls the carnal act "knowing.") He is their worst enemy to the extent that he is ignorant of them. A chronicler relates that the true *Burlador* died assassinated by Franciscans who wanted "to put an end to the excesses and blasphemies of Don Juan, whose birth assured him impunity." Then they proclaimed that heaven had struck him down. No one has proved that strange end. Nor has anyone proved the contrary. But without wondering if it is probable, I can say that it is logical. I want merely to single out at this point the word "birth" and to play on words: it was the fact of living that assured his innocence. It was from death alone that he derived a guilt now become legendary.

What else does that stone Commander signify, that cold statue set in motion to punish the blood and courage that dared to think? All the powers of eternal Reason, of order, of universal morality, all the foreign grandeur of a God open to wrath are summed up in him. That gigantic and soulless stone merely symbolizes the forces that Don Juan negated forever. But the Commander's mission stops there. The thunder and lightning can return to the imitation heaven whence they were called forth. The real tragedy takes place quite apart from them. No, it was not under a stone hand that Don Juan met his death. I am inclined to believe in the legendary bravado, in that mad laughter of the healthy man provoking a non-existent God. But, above all, I believe that on that evening when Don Juan was waiting at Anna's the Commander didn't come, and that after midnight the blasphemer must have felt the dreadful bitterness of those who have been right. I accept even more readily the account of his life that has him eventually burying himself in a monastery. Not that the edifying aspect of the story can be considered probable. What refuge can he go ask of God? But this symbolizes rather the logical outcome of a life completely imbued with the absurd, the grim ending of an existence turned toward short-lived joys. At this point sensual pleasure winds up in asceticism. It is essential to realize that they may be, as it were, the two aspects of the same destitution. What more ghastly image can be called up than that of a man betrayed by his body who, simply because he did not die in time, lives out the comedy while awaiting the end, face to face with that God he does not adore, serving him as he served life, kneeling before a void and arms outstretched toward a heaven without eloquence that he knows to be also without depth?

I see Don Juan in a cell of one of those Spanish monasteries lost on a hilltop. And if he contemplates anything at all, it is not the ghosts of past loves, but perhaps, through a narrow slit in the sun-baked wall, some silent Spanish plain, a noble, soulless land in which he recognizes himself. Yes, it is on this melancholy and radiant image that the curtain must be rung down. The ultimate end, awaited but never desired, the ultimate end is negligible.

Drama

"The play's the thing," says Hamlet, "wherein I'll catch the conscience of the king." "Catch" is indeed the word. For conscience moves swiftly or withdraws within itself. It has to be caught on the wing, at that barely perceptible moment when it glances fleetingly at itself. The everyday man does not enjoy tarrying. Everything, on the contrary, hurries him onward. But at the same time nothing interests him more than himself, especially his potentialities. Whence his interest in the theater, in the show, where so many fates are offered him, where he can accept the poetry without feeling the sorrow. There at least can be recognized the thoughtless man, and he continues to hasten toward some hope or other. The absurd man begins where that one leaves off, where, ceasing to admire the play, the mind wants to enter in. Entering into all these lives, experiencing them in their diversity, amounts to acting them out. I am not saying that actors in general obey that impulse, that they are absurd men, but that their fate is an absurd fate which might charm and attract a lucid heart. It is necessary to establish this in order to grasp without misunderstanding what will follow.

The actor's realm is that of the fleeting. Of all kinds of fame, it is known, his is the most ephemeral. At least, this is said in conversation. But all kinds of fame are ephemeral. From the point of view of Sirius, Goethe's works in ten thousand years will be dust and his name forgotten. Perhaps a handful of archæologists will look for "evidence" as to our era. That idea has always contained a lesson. Seriously meditated upon, it reduces our perturbations to the profound nobility that is found in indifference. Above all, it directs our concerns toward what is most certain—that is, toward the immediate. Of all kinds of fame the least deceptive is the one that is lived.

Hence the actor has chosen multiple fame, the fame that is hallowed and tested. From the fact that everything is to die someday he draws the best conclusion. An actor succeeds or does not succeed. A writer has some hope even if he is not appreciated. He assumes that his works will bear witness to what he was. At best the actor will leave us a photograph, and nothing of what he was himself, his gestures and his silences, his gasping or his panting with love, will come down to us. For him, not to be known is not to act, and not acting is dying a hundred times with all the creatures he would have brought to life or resuscitated.

Why should we be surprised to find a fleeting fame built upon the most ephemeral of creations? The actor has three hours to be Iago or Alceste, Phèdre or Gloucester. In that short space of time he makes them come to life and die on fifty square yards of boards. Never has the absurd been so well illustrated or at such length. What more revelatory epitome can be imagined than those marvelous lives, those exceptional and total destinies unfolding for a few hours within a stage set? Off the stage, Sigismundo ceases to count. Two hours later he is seen dining out. Then it is, perhaps, that life is a dream. But after Sigismundo comes another. The hero suffering from uncertainty takes the place of the man roaring for his revenge. By thus sweeping over centuries and minds, by miming man as he can be and as he is, the actor has much in common with that other absurd individual, the traveler. Like him, he drains something and is constantly on the move. He is a traveler in time and, for the best, the hunted traveler, pursued by souls. If ever the ethics of quantity could find sustenance, it is indeed on that strange stage. To what degree the actor benefits from the characters is hard to say. But that is not the important thing. It is merely a matter of knowing how far he identifies himself with those irreplaceable lives. It often happens that he carries them with him, that they somewhat overflow the time and place in which they were born. They accompany the actor, who cannot very readily separate himself from what he has been. Occasionally when reaching for his glass he resumes Hamlet's gesture of raising his cup. No, the distance separating him from the creatures into whom he infuses life is not so great. He abundantly illustrates every month or every day that so suggestive truth that there is no frontier between what a man wants to be and what he is. Always concerned with better representing, he demonstrates to what a degree appearing creates being. For that is his art—to simulate absolutely, to project himself as deeply as possible into lives that are not his own. At the end of his effort his vocation becomes clear: to apply himself wholeheartedly to being nothing or to being several. The narrower the limits allotted him for creating his character, the more necessary his talent. He will die in three hours under the mask he has assumed today. Within three hours he must experience and express a whole exceptional life. That is called losing oneself to find oneself. In those three hours he travels the whole course of the dead-end path that the man in the audience takes a lifetime to cover.

A mime of the ephemeral, the actor trains and perfects himself only in appearances. The theatrical convention is that the heart expresses itself and communicates itself only through gestures and in the body—or through the voice, which is as much of the soul as of the body. The rule of that art insists that everything be magnified and translated into flesh. If it were essential on the stage to love as people really love, to employ that irreplaceable voice of the heart, to look as people contemplate in life, our speech would be in code. But here silences must make themselves heard. Love speaks up louder, and immobility itself becomes spectacular. The body is king. Not everyone can be "theatrical," and this unjustly maligned word covers a whole æsthetic and a whole ethic. Half a man's life is spent in implying, in turning away, and in keeping silent. Here the actor is the intruder. He breaks the spell chaining that soul, and at last the passions can rush onto their stage. They speak in every gesture; they live only through shouts and cries. Thus the actor creates his characters for display. He outlines or sculptures them and slips into their imaginary form, transfusing his blood into their phantoms. I am of course speaking of great drama, the kind that gives the actor an *opportunity* to fulfill his wholly physical fate. Take Shakespeare, for instance. In that impulsive drama the physical passions lead the dance. They explain everything. Without them all would collapse. Never would King Lear keep the appointment set by madness without the brutal gesture that exiles Cordelia and condemns Edgar. It is just that the unfolding of that tragedy should thenceforth be dominated by madness. Souls are given over to the demons and their saraband. No fewer than four madmen: one by trade, another by intention, and the last two through suffering —four disordered bodies, four unutterable aspects of a single condition.

The very scale of the human body is inadequate. The mask and the buskin, the make-up that reduces and accentuates the face in its essential elements, the costume that exaggerates and simplifies—that universe sacrifices everything to appearance and is made solely for the eye. Through an absurd miracle, it is the body that also brings knowledge. I should never really understand Iago unless I played his part. It is not enough to hear him, for I grasp him only at the moment when I see him. Of the absurd character the actor consequently has the monotony, that single, oppressive silhouette, simultaneously strange and familiar, that he carries about from hero to hero. There, too, the great dramatic work contributes to this unity of tone.[2] This is where the actor contradicts himself: the same and yet so various, so many souls summed up in a single body. Yet it is the absurd contradiction itself, that individual who wants to achieve everything and live everything, that useless attempt, that ineffectual persistence. What always contradicts itself nevertheless joins in him. He is at that point where body and mind converge, where the mind, tired of its defeats, turns toward its most faithful ally. "And blest are those," says Hamlet, "whose blood and judgment are so well commingled that they are not a pipe for fortune's finger to sound what stop she please."

How could the Church have failed to condemn such a practice on the part of the actor? She repudiated in that art the heretical multiplication of souls, the emotional debauch, the scandalous presumption of a mind that objects to living but one life and hurls itself into all forms of excess. She proscribed in them that preference for the present and that triumph of Proteus which are the negation of everything she teaches. Eternity is not a game. A mind foolish enough to prefer a comedy to eternity has lost its salvation. Between "everywhere" and "forever" there is no compromise. Whence that much maligned profession can give rise to a tremendous spiritual conflict. "What matters," said Nietzsche, "is not eternal life but eternal vivacity." All drama is, in fact, in this choice.

Adrienne Lecouvreur on her deathbed was willing to confess and receive communion, but refused to abjure her profession. She thereby lost the benefit of the confession. Did this not amount, in effect, to choosing her absorbing passion in preference to God? And that woman in the death throes refusing in tears to repudiate what she called her art gave evidence of a greatness that she never achieved behind the footlights. This was her finest role and the hardest one to play. Choosing between

[2] At this point I am thinking of Molière's Alceste. Everything is so simple, so obvious and so coarse. Alceste against Philinte, Célimène against Elianthe, the whole subject in the absurd consequence of a nature carried to its extreme, and the verse itself, the "bad verse," barely accented like the monotony of the character's nature.

heaven and a ridiculous fidelity, preferring oneself to eternity or losing oneself in God is the age-old tragedy in which each must play his part.

The actors of the era knew they were excommunicated. Entering the profession amounted to choosing Hell. And the Church discerned in them her worst enemies. A few men of letters protest: "What! Refuse the last rites to Molière!" But that was just, and especially in one who died onstage and finished under the actor's make-up a life entirely devoted to dispersion. In his case genius is invoked, which excuses everything. But genius excuses nothing, just because it refuses to do so.

The actor knew at that time what punishment was in store for him. But what significance could such vague threats have compared to the final punishment that life itself was reserving for him? This was the one that he felt in advance and accepted wholly. To the actor as to the absurd man, a premature death is irreparable. Nothing can make up for the sum of faces and centuries he would otherwise have traversed. But in any case, one has to die. For the actor is doubtless everywhere, but time sweeps him along, too, and makes its impression with him.

It requires but a little imagination to feel what an actor's fate means. It is in time that he makes up and enumerates his characters. It is in time likewise that he learns to dominate them. The greater number of different lives he has lived, the more aloof he can be from them. The time comes when he must die to the stage and for the world. What he has lived faces him. He sees clearly. He feels the harrowing and irreplaceable quality of that adventure. He knows and can now die. There are homes for aged actors.

Conquest

"No," says the conqueror, "don't assume that because I love action I have had to forget how to think. On the contrary I can thoroughly define what I believe. For I believe it firmly and I see it surely and clearly. Beware of those who say: 'I know this too well to be able to express it.' For if they cannot do so, this is because they don't know it or because out of laziness they stopped at the outer crust.

"I have not many opinions. At the end of a life man notices that he has spent years becoming sure of a single truth. But a single truth, if it is obvious, is enough to guide an existence. As for me, I decidedly have something to say about the individual. One must speak of him bluntly and, if need be, with the appropriate contempt.

"A man is more a man through the things he keeps to himself than through those he says. There are many that I shall keep to myself. But I firmly believe that all those who have judged the individual have done so with much less experience than we on which to base their judgment. The intelligence, the stirring intelligence perhaps foresaw what it was essential to note. But the era, its ruins, and its blood overwhelm us with facts. It was possible for ancient nations, and even for more recent ones down to our machine age, to weigh one against the other the virtues of society and of the individual, to try to find out which was to serve the other. To begin with, that was possible by virtue of that stubborn aberration in man's heart according to which human beings were created to serve or be served. In the second place, it was possible because neither society nor the individual had yet revealed all their ability.

"I have seen bright minds express astonishment at the masterpieces of Dutch painters born at the height of the bloody wars in Flanders, be amazed by the prayers of Silesian mystics brought up during the frightful Thirty Years' War. Eternal values survive secular turmoils before their astonished eyes. But there has been progress since. The painters of today are deprived of such serenity. Even if they have basically the heart the creator needs—I mean the closed heart—it is of no use; for everyone, including the saint himself, is mobilized. This is perhaps what I have felt most deeply. At every form that miscarries in the trenches, at every outline, metaphor, or prayer crushed under steel, the eternal loses a round. Conscious that I cannot stand aloof from my time, I have decided to be an integral part of it. This is why I esteem the individual only because he strikes me as ridiculous and humiliated. Knowing that there are no victorious causes, I have a liking for lost causes: they require an uncontaminated soul, equal to its defeat as to its temporary victories. For anyone who feels bound up with this world's fate, the clash of civilizations has something agonizing about it. I have made that anguish mine at the same time that I wanted to join in. Between history and the eternal I have chosen history because I like certainties. Of it, at least, I am certain, and how can I deny this force crushing me?

"There always comes a time when one must choose between contemplation and action. This is called becoming a man. Such wrenches are dreadful. But for a proud heart there can be no compromise. There is God or time, that cross or this sword. This world has a higher meaning that transcends its worries, or nothing is true but those worries. One must live with time and die with it, or else elude it for a greater life. I know that one can compromise and live in the world while believing in the eternal. That is called accepting. But I loathe this term and want all or nothing. If I choose action, don't think that contemplation is like an unknown country to me. But it cannot give me everything, and, deprived of the eternal, I want to ally myself with time. I do not want to put down to my account either nostalgia or bitterness, and I merely want to see clearly. I tell you, tomorrow you will be mobilized. For you and for me that is a liberation. The individual can do nothing and yet he can do everything. In that wonderful unattached state you understand why I exalt and crush him at one and the same time. It is the world that pulverizes him and I who liberate him. I provide him with all his rights.

"Conquerors know that action is in itself useless. There is but one useful action, that of remaking man and the earth. I shall never remake men. But one must do 'as if.' For the path of struggle leads me to the flesh. Even humiliated, the flesh is my only certainty. I can live only on it. The creature is my native land. This is why I have chosen this absurd and ineffectual effort.

This is why I am on the side of the struggle. The epoch lends itself to this, as I have said. Hitherto the greatness of a conqueror was geographical. It was measured by the extent of the conquered territories. There is a reason why the word has changed in meaning and has ceased to signify the victorious general. The greatness has changed camp. It lies in protest and the blind-alley sacrifice. There, too, it is not through a preference for defeat. Victory would be desirable. But there is but one victory, and it is eternal. That is the one I shall never have. That is where I stumble and cling. A revolution is always accomplished against the gods, beginning with the revolution of Prometheus, the first of modern conquerors. It is man's demands made against his fate; the demands of the poor are but a pretext. Yet I can seize that spirit only in its historical act, and that is where I make contact with it. Don't assume, however, that I take pleasure in it: opposite the essential contradiction, I maintain my human contradiction. I establish my lucidity in the midst of what negates it. I exalt man before what crushes him, and my freedom, my revolt, and my passion come together then in that tension, that lucidity, and that vast repetition.

"Yes, man is his own end. And he is his only end. If he aims to be something, it is in this life. Now I know it only too well. Conquerors sometimes talk of vanquishing and overcoming. But it is always 'overcoming oneself' that they mean. You are well aware of what that means. Every man has felt himself to be the equal of a god at certain moments. At least, this is the way it is expressed. But this comes from the fact that in a flash he felt the amazing grandeur of the human mind. The conquerors are merely those among men who are conscious enough of their strength to be sure of living constantly on those heights and fully aware of that grandeur. It is a question of arithmetic, of more or less. The conquerors are capable of the more. But they are capable of no more than man himself when he wants. This is why they never leave the human crucible, plunging into the seething soul of revolutions.

"There they find the creature mutilated, but they also encounter there the only values they like and admire, man and his silence. This is both their destitution and their wealth. There is but one luxury for them—that of human relations. How can one fail to realize that in this vulnerable universe everything that is human and solely human assumes a more vivid meaning? Taut faces, threatened fraternity, such strong and chaste friendship among men—these are the true riches because they are transitory. In their midst the mind is most aware of its powers and limitations. That is to say, its efficacy. Some have spoken of genius. But genius is easy to say; I prefer the intelligence. It must be said that it can be magnificent then. It lights up this desert and dominates it. It knows its obligations and illustrates them. It will die at the same time as this body. But knowing this constitutes its freedom.

"We are not ignorant of the fact that all churches are against us. A heart so keyed up eludes the eternal, and all churches, divine or political, lay claim to the eternal. Happiness and courage, retribution or justice are secondary ends for them. It is a doctrine they bring, and one must subscribe to it. But I have no concern with ideas or with the eternal. The truths that come within my scope can be touched with the hand. I cannot separate from them. This is why you cannot base anything on me: nothing of the conqueror lasts, not even his doctrines.

"At the end of all that, despite everything, is death. We know also that it ends everything. This is why those cemeteries all over Europe, which obsess some among us, are hideous. People beautify only what they love, and death repels us and tires our patience. It, too, is to be conquered. The last Carrara, a prisoner in Padua emptied by the plague and besieged by the Venetians, ran screaming through the halls of his deserted palace: he was calling on the devil and asking him for death. This was a way of overcoming it. And it is likewise a mark of courage characteristic of the Occident to have made so ugly the places where death thinks itself honored. In the rebel's universe, death exalts injustice. It is the supreme abuse.

"Others, without compromising either, have chosen the eternal and denounced the illusion of this world. Their cemeteries smile amid numerous flowers and birds.

That suits the conqueror and gives him a clear image of what he has rejected. He has chosen, on the contrary, the black iron fence or the potter's field. The best among the men of God occasionally are seized with fright mingled with consideration and pity for minds that can live with such an image of their death. Yet those minds derive their strength and justification from this. Our fate stands before us and we provoke him. Less out of pride than out of awareness of our ineffectual condition. We, too, sometimes feel pity for ourselves. It is the only compassion that seems acceptable to us: a feeling that perhaps you hardly understand and that seems to you scarcely virile. Yet the most daring among us are the ones who feel it. But we call the lucid ones virile and we do not want a strength that is apart from lucidity."

Let me repeat that these images do not propose moral codes and involve no judgments: they are sketches. They merely represent a style of life. The lover, the actor, or the adventurer plays the absurd. But equally well, if he wishes, the chaste man, the civil servant, or the president of the Republic. It is enough to know and to mask nothing. In Italian museums are sometimes found little painted screens that the priest used to hold in front of the face of condemned men to hide the scaffold from them. The leap in all its forms, rushing into the divine or the eternal, surrendering to the illusions of the everyday or of the idea —all these screens hide the absurd. But there are civil servants without screens, and they are the ones of whom I mean to speak.

I have chosen the most extreme ones. At this level the absurd gives them a royal power. It is true that those princes are without a kingdom. But they have this advantage over others: they know that all royalties are illusory. They know that is their whole nobility, and it is useless to speak in relation to them of hidden misfortune or the ashes of disillusion. Being deprived of hope is not despairing. The flames of earth are surely worth celestial perfumes. Neither I nor anyone can judge them here. They are not striving to be better; they are attempting to be consistent. If the term "wise man" can be applied to the man who lives on what he has without speculating on what he has not, then they are wise men. One of them, a conqueror but in the realm of mind, a Don Juan but of knowledge, an actor but of the intelligence, knows this better than anyone: "You nowise deserve a privilege on earth and in heaven for having brought to perfection your dear little meek sheep; you nonetheless continue to be at best a ridiculous dear little sheep with horns and nothing more—even supposing that you do not burst with vanity and do not create a scandal by posing as a judge."

In any case, it was essential to restore to the absurd reasoning more cordial examples. The imagination can add many others, inseparable from time and exile, who likewise know how to live in harmony with a universe without future and without weakness. This absurd, godless world is, then, peopled with men who think clearly and have ceased to hope. And I have not yet spoken of the most absurd character, who is the creator.

Absurd Creation

*

Philosophy and Fiction

All those lives maintained in the rarefied air of the absurd could not persevere without some profound and constant thought to infuse its strength into them. Right here, it can be only a strange feeling of fidelity. Conscious men have been seen to fulfill their task amid the most stupid of wars without considering themselves in contradiction. This is because it was essential to elude nothing. There is thus a metaphysical honor in enduring the world's absurdity. Conquest or play-acting, multiple loves, absurd revolt are tributes that man pays to his dignity in a campaign in which he is defeated in advance.

It is merely a matter of being faithful to the rule of the battle. That thought may suffice to sustain a mind; it has supported and still supports whole civilizations. War cannot be negated. One must live it or die of it. So it is with the absurd: it is a question of breathing with it, of recognizing its lessons and recovering their flesh. In this regard the absurd joy par excellence is creation. "Art and nothing but art," said Nietzsche; "we have art in order not to die of the truth."

In the experience that I am attempting to describe and to stress on several modes, it is certain that a new torment arises wherever another dies. The childish chasing after forgetfulness, the appeal of satisfaction are now devoid of echo. But the constant tension that keeps man face to face with the world, the ordered delirium that urges him to be receptive to everything leave him another fever. In this universe the work of art is then the sole chance of keeping his consciousness and of fixing its adventures. Creating is living doubly. The groping, anxious quest of a Proust, his meticulous collecting of flowers, of wallpapers, and of anxieties, signifies nothing else. At the same time, it has no more significance than the continual and imperceptible creation in which the actor, the conqueror, and all absurd men indulge every day of their lives. All try their hands at miming, at repeating, and at re-creating the reality that is theirs. We always end up by having the appearance of our truths. All existence for a man turned away from the eternal is but a vast mime under the mask of the absurd. Creation is the great mime.

Such men know to begin with, and then their whole effort is to examine, to enlarge, and to enrich the ephemeral island on which they have just landed. But first they must know. For the absurd discovery coincides with a pause in which future passions are prepared and justified. Even men without a gospel have their Mount of Olives. And one must not fall asleep on theirs either. For the absurd man it is not a matter of explaining and solving, but of experiencing and describing. Everything begins with lucid indifference.

Describing—that is the last ambition of an absurd thought. Science likewise, having reached the end of its paradoxes, ceases to propound and stops to contemplate and sketch the ever virgin landscape of phenomena. The heart learns thus that the emotion delighting us when we see the world's aspects comes to us not from its depth but from their diversity. Explanation is useless, but the sensation remains and, with it, the constant attractions of a universe inexhaustible in quantity. The place of the work of art can be understood at this point.

It marks both the death of an experience and its multiplication. It is a sort of monotonous and passionate repetition of the themes already orchestrated by the world: the body, inexhaustible image on the pediment of temples, forms or colors, number or grief. It is therefore not indifferent, as a conclusion, to encounter once again the principal themes of this essay in the wonderful and childish world of the creator. It would be wrong to see a symbol in it and to think that the work of art can be considered at last as a refuge for the absurd. It is itself an absurd phenomenon, and we are concerned merely with its description. It does not offer an escape for the intellectual ailment. Rather, it is one of the symptoms of that ailment which reflects it throughout a man's whole thought. But for the first time it makes the mind get outside of itself and places it in opposition to others, not for it to get lost but to show it clearly the blind path that all have entered upon. In the time of the absurd reasoning, creation follows indifference and discovery. It marks the point from which absurd passions spring and where the reasoning stops. Its place in this essay is justified in this way.

It will suffice to bring to light a few themes common to the creator and the thinker in order to find in the work of art all the contradictions of thought involved in the absurd. Indeed, it is not so much identical conclusions that prove minds to be related as the contradictions that are common to them. So it is with thought and creation. I hardly need to say that the same anguish urges man to these two attitudes. This is where they coincide in the beginning. But among all the thoughts that start from the absurd, I have seen that very few remain within it. And through their deviations or infidelities I have best been able to measure what belonged to the absurd. Similarly I must wonder: is an absurd work of art possible?

It would be impossible to insist too much on the arbitrary nature of the former opposition between art and philosophy. If you insist on taking it in too limited a sense, it is certainly false. If you mean merely that these two disciplines each have their peculiar climate, that is probably true but remains vague. The only acceptable argument used to lie in the contradiction brought up between the philosopher enclosed *within* his system and the artist placed *before* his work. But this was pertinent for a certain form of art and of philosophy which we consider secondary here. The idea of an art detached from its creator is not only outmoded; it is false. In opposition to the artist, it is pointed out that no philosopher ever created several systems. But that is true in so far, indeed, as no artist ever expressed more than one thing under different aspects. The instantaneous perfection of art, the necessity for its renewal—this is true only through a preconceived notion. For the work of art likewise is a construction and everyone knows how monotonous the great creators can be. For the same reason as the thinker, the artist commits himself and becomes himself in his work. That osmosis raises the most important of æsthetic problems. Moreover, to anyone who is convinced of the mind's singleness of purpose, nothing is more futile than these distinctions based on methods and objects. There are no frontiers between the disciplines that man sets himself for understanding and loving. They interlock, and the same anxiety merges them.

It is necessary to state this to begin with. For an absurd work of art to be possible, thought in its most lucid form must be involved in it. But at the same time thought must not be apparent except as the regulating intelligence. This paradox can be explained according to the absurd. The work of art is born of the intelligence's refusal to reason the concrete. It marks the triumph of the carnal. It is lucid thought that provokes it, but in that very act that thought repudiates itself. It will not yield to the temptation of adding to what is described a deeper meaning that it knows to be illegitimate. The work of art embodies a drama of the intelligence, but it proves this only indirectly. The absurd work requires an artist conscious of these limitations and an art in which the concrete signifies nothing more than itself. It cannot be the end, the meaning, and the consolation of a life. Creating or not creating changes nothing. The absurd creator does not prize his work. He could repudiate it. He does sometimes repudiate it. An Abyssinia suffices for this, as in the case of Rimbaud.

At the same time a rule of æsthetics can be seen in this. The true work of art is always on the human scale. It is essentially the one that says "less." There is a certain relationship between the global experience of the artist and the work that reflects that experience, between *Wilhelm Meister* and Goethe's maturity. That relationship is bad when the work aims to give the whole experience in the lace-paper of an explanatory literature. That relationship is good when the work is but a piece cut out of experience, a facet of the diamond in which the inner luster is epitomized without being limited. In the first case there is overloading and pretension to the eternal. In the second, a fecund work because of a whole implied experience, the wealth of which is suspected. The problem for the absurd artist is to acquire this *savoir-vivre* which transcends *savoir-faire.* And in the end, the great artist under this climate is, above all, a great living being, it being understood that living in this case is just as much experiencing as reflecting. The work then embodies an intellectual drama. The absurd work illustrates thought's renouncing of its prestige and its resignation to being no more than the intelligence that works up appearances and covers with images what has no reason. If the world were clear, art would not exist.

I am not speaking here of the arts of form or color in which description alone prevails in its splendid modesty.[1] Expression begins where thought ends. Those adolescents with empty eyesockets who people temples and museums —their philosophy has been expressed in gestures. For an absurd man it is more educative than all libraries. Under another aspect the same is true for music. If any art is devoid of lessons, it is certainly music. It is too closely related to mathematics not to have borrowed their gratuitousness. That game the mind plays with itself according to set and measured laws takes place in the sonorous compass that belongs to us and beyond which the vibrations nevertheless meet in an inhuman universe. There is no purer sensation. These examples are too easy. The absurd man recognizes as his own these harmonies and these forms.

But I should like to speak here of a work in which the temptation to explain remains greatest, in which illusion offers itself automatically, in which conclusion is almost inevitable. I mean fictional creation. I propose to inquire whether or not the absurd can hold its own there.

---

[1] It is curious to note that the most intellectual kind of painting, the one that tries to reduce reality to its essential elements, is ultimately but a visual delight. All it has kept of the world is its color. (This is apparent particularly in Léger.)

To think is first of all to create a world (or to limit one's own world, which comes to the same thing). It is starting out from the basic disagreement that separates man from his experience in order to find a common ground according to one's nostalgia, a universe hedged with reasons or lighted up with analogies but which, in any case, gives an opportunity to rescind the unbearable divorce. The philosopher, even if he is Kant, is a creator. He has his characters, his symbols, and his secret action. He has his plot endings. On the contrary, the lead taken by the novel over poetry and the essay merely represents, despite appearances, a greater intellectualization of the art. Let there be no mistake about it; I am speaking of the greatest. The fecundity and the importance of a literary form are often measured by the trash it contains. The number of bad novels must not make us forget the value of the best. These, indeed, carry with them their universe. The novel has its logic, its reasonings, its intuition, and its postulates. It also has its requirements of clarity.[2]

The classical opposition of which I was speaking above is even less justified in this particular case. It held in the time when it was easy to separate philosophy from its authors. Today when thought has ceased to lay claim to the universal, when its best history would be that of its repentances, we know that the system, when it is worth while, cannot be separated from its author. The *Ethics* itself, in one of its aspects, is but a long and reasoned personal confession. Abstract thought at last returns to its prop of flesh. And, likewise, the fictional activities of the body and of the passions are regulated a little more according to the requirements of a vision of the world. The writer has given up telling "stories" and creates his universe. The great novelists are philosophical novelists—that is, the contrary of thesis-writers. For instance, Balzac,

[2] If you stop to think of it, this explains the worst novels. Almost everybody considers himself capable of thinking and, to a certain degree, whether right or wrong, really does think. Very few, on the contrary, can fancy themselves poets or artists in words. But from the moment when thought won out over style, the mob invaded the novel.

That is not such a great evil as is said. The best are led to make greater demands upon themselves. As for those who succumb, they did not deserve to survive.

Sade, Melville, Stendhal, Dostoevsky, Proust, Malraux, Kafka, to cite but a few.

But in fact the preference they have shown for writing in images rather than in reasoned arguments is revelatory of a certain thought that is common to them all, convinced of the uselessness of any principle of explanation and sure of the educative message of perceptible appearance. They consider the work of art both as an end and a beginning. It is the outcome of an often unexpressed philosophy, its illustration and its consummation. But it is complete only through the implications of that philosophy. It justifies at last that variant of an old theme that a little thought estranges from life whereas much thought reconciles to life. Incapable of refining the real, thought pauses to mimic it. The novel in question is the instrument of that simultaneously relative and inexhaustible knowledge, so like that of love. Of love, fictional creation has the inital wonder and the fecund rumination.

These at least are the charms I see in it at the outset. But I saw them likewise in those princes of humiliated thought whose suicides I was later able to witness. What interests me, indeed, is knowing and describing the force that leads them back toward the common path of illusion. The same method will consequently help me here. The fact of having already utilized it will allow me to shorten my argument and to sum it up without delay in a particular example. I want to know whether, accepting a life *without appeal*, one can also agree to work and create *without appeal* and what is the way leading to these liberties. I want to liberate my universe of its phantoms and to people it solely with flesh-and-blood truths whose presence I cannot deny. I can perform absurd work, choose the creative attitude rather than another. But an absurd attitude, if it is to remain so, must remain aware of its gratuitousness. So it is with the work of art. If the commandments of the absurd are not respected, if the work does not illustrate divorce and revolt, if it sacrifices to illusions and arouses hope, it ceases to be gratuitous. I can no longer detach myself from it. My life may find a meaning in it, but that is trifling. It ceases to be that exercise in detachment and passion which crowns the splendor and futility of a man's life.

In the creation in which the temptation to explain is the strongest, can one overcome that temptation? In the fictional world in which awareness of the real world is keenest, can I remain faithful to the absurd without sacrificing to the desire to judge? So many questions to be taken into consideration in a last effort. It must be already clear what they signify. They are the last scruples of an awareness that fears to forsake its initial and difficult lesson in favor of a final illusion. What holds for creation, looked upon as *one* of the possible attitudes for the man conscious of the absurd, holds for all the styles of life open to him. The conqueror or the actor, the creator or Don Juan may forget that their exercise in living could not do without awareness of its mad character. One becomes accustomed so quickly. A man wants to earn money in order to be happy, and his whole effort and the best of a life are devoted to the earning of that money. Happiness is forgotten; the means are taken for the end. Likewise, the whole effort of this conqueror will be diverted to ambition, which was but a way toward a greater life. Don Juan in turn will likewise yield to his fate, be satisfied with that existence whose nobility is of value only through revolt. For one it is awareness and for the other, revolt; in both cases the absurd has disappeared. There is so much stubborn hope in the human heart. The most destitute men often end up by accepting illusion. That approval prompted by the need for peace inwardly parallels the existential consent. There are thus gods of light and idols of mud. But it is essential to find the middle path leading to the faces of man.

So far, the failures of the absurd exigence have best informed us as to what it is. In the same way, if we are to be informed, it will suffice to notice that fictional creation can present the same ambiguity as certain philosophies. Hence I can choose as illustration a work comprising everything that denotes awareness of the absurd, having a clear starting-point and a lucid climate. Its consequences will enlighten us. If the absurd is not respected in it, we shall know by what expedient illusion enters in. A particular example, a theme, a creator's fidelity will suffice, then. This involves the same analysis that has already been made at greater length.

I shall examine a favorite theme of Dostoevsky. I might just as well have studied other works.[3] But in this work the problem is treated directly, in the sense of nobility and emotion, as for the existential philosophies already discussed. This parallelism serves my purpose.

Kirilov

All of Dostoevsky's heroes question themselves as to the meaning of life. In this they are modern: they do not fear ridicule. What distinguishes modern sensibility from classical sensibility is that the latter thrives on moral problems and the former on metaphysical problems. In Dostoevsky's novels the question is propounded with such intensity that it can only invite extreme solutions. Existence is illusory *or* it is eternal. If Dostoevsky were satisfied with this inquiry, he would be a philosopher. But he illustrates the consequences that such intellectual pastimes may have in a man's life, and in this regard he is an artist. Among those consequences, his attention is arrested particularly by the last one, which he himself calls logical suicide in his *Diary of a Writer*. In the installments for December 1876, indeed, he imagines the reasoning of "logical suicide." Convinced that human existence is an utter absurdity for anyone without faith in immortality, the desperate man comes to the following conclusions:

"Since in reply to my questions about happiness, I am told, through the intermediary of my consciousness, that I cannot be happy except in harmony with the great all, which I cannot conceive and shall never be in a position to conceive, it is evident . . ."

"Since, finally, in this connection, I assume both the role of the plaintiff and that of the defendant, of the

[3] Malraux's work, for instance. But it would have been necessary to deal at the same time with the social question which in fact cannot be avoided by absurd thought (even though that thought may put forward several solutions, very different from one another). One must, however, limit oneself.

accused and of the judge, and since I consider this comedy perpetrated by nature altogether stupid, and since I even deem it humiliating for me to deign to play it . . ."

"In my indisputable capacity of plaintiff and defendant, of judge and accused, I condemn that nature which, with such impudent nerve, brought me into being in order to suffer—I condemn it to be annihilated with me."

There remains a little humor in that position. This suicide kills himself because, on the metaphysical plane, he is *vexed*. In a certain sense he is taking his revenge. This is his way of proving that he "will not be had." It is known, however, that the same theme is embodied, but with the most wonderful generality, in Kirilov of *The Possessed*, likewise an advocate of logical suicide. Kirilov the engineer declares somewhere that he wants to take his own life because it "is his idea." Obviously the word must be taken in its proper sense. It is for an idea, a thought, that he is getting ready for death. This is the superior suicide. Progressively, in a series of scenes in which Kirilov's mask is gradually illuminated, the fatal thought driving him is revealed to us. The engineer, in fact, goes back to the arguments of the *Diary*. He feels that God is necessary and that he must exist. But he knows that he does not and cannot exist. "Why do you not realize," he exclaims, "that this is sufficient reason for killing oneself?" That attitude involves likewise for him some of the absurd consequences. Through indifference he accepts letting his suicide be used to the advantage of a cause he despises. "I decided last night that I didn't care." And finally he prepares his deed with a mixed feeling of revolt and freedom. "I shall kill myself in order to assert my insubordination, my new and dreadful liberty." It is no longer a question of revenge, but of revolt. Kirilov is consequently an absurd character—yet with this essential reservation: he kills himself. But he himself explains this contradiction, and in such a way that at the same time he reveals the absurd secret in all its purity. In truth, he adds to his fatal logic an extraordinary ambition which gives the character its full perspective: he wants to kill himself to become god.

The reasoning is classic in its clarity. If God does not exist, Kirilov is god. If God does not exist, Kirilov must

kill himself. Kirilov must therefore kill himself to become god. That logic is absurd, but it is what is needed.
The interesting thing, however, is to give a meaning to
that divinity brought to earth. That amounts to clarify-
ing the premise: "If God does not exist, I am god,"
which still remains rather obscure. It is important to
note at the outset that the man who flaunts that mad
claim is indeed of this world. He performs his gymnas-
tics every morning to preserve his health. He is stirred
by the joy of Chatov recovering his wife. On a sheet of
paper to be found after his death he wants to draw a face
sticking out his tongue at "them." He is childish and
irascible, passionate, methodical, and sensitive. Of the
superman he has nothing but the logic and the obses-
sion, whereas of man he has the whole catalogue. Yet
it is he who speaks calmly of his divinity. He is not mad,
or else Dostoevsky is. Consequently it is not a megalo-
maniac's illusion that excites him. And taking the words
in their specific sense would, in this instance, be ridiculous.

Kirilov himself helps us to understand. In reply to a
question from Stavrogin, he makes clear that he is not
talking of a god-man. It might be thought that this
springs from concern to distinguish himself from Christ.
But in reality it is a matter of annexing Christ. Kirilov
in fact fancies for a moment that Jesus at his death *did
not find himself in Paradise*. He found out then that
his torture had been useless. "The laws of nature," says
the engineer, "made Christ live in the midst of falsehood and die for a falsehood." Solely in this sense Jesus
indeed personifies the whole human drama. He is the
complete man, being the one who realized the most
absurd condition. He is not the God-man but the man-
god. And, like him, each of us can be crucified and
victimized—and is to a certain degree.

The divinity in question is therefore altogether terrestrial. "For three years," says Kirilov, "I sought the
attribute of my divinity and I have found it. The attribute of my divinity is independence." Now can be
seen the meaning of Kirilov's premise: "If God does not
exist, I am god." To become god is merely to be free on
this earth, not to serve an immortal being. Above all, of

course, it is drawing all the inferences from that painful independence. If God exists, all depends on him and we can do nothing against his will. If he does not exist, everything depends on us. For Kirilov, as for Nietzsche, to kill God is to become god oneself; it is to realize on this earth the eternal life of which the Gospel speaks.[4]

But if this metaphysical crime is enough for man's fulfillment, why add suicide? Why kill oneself and leave this world after having won freedom? That is contradictory. Kirilov is well aware of this, for he adds: "If you feel *that*, you are a tsar and, far from killing yourself, you will live covered with glory." But men in general do not know it. They do not feel "that." As in the time of Prometheus, they entertain blind hopes.[5] They need to be shown the way and cannot do without preaching. Consequently, Kirilov must kill himself out of love for humanity. He must show his brothers a royal and difficult path on which he will be the first. It is a pedagogical suicide. Kirilov sacrifices himself, then. But if he is crucified, he will not be victimized. He remains the man-god, convinced of a death without future, imbued with evangelical melancholy. "I," he says, "am unhappy because I am *obliged* to assert my freedom." But once he is dead and men are at last enlightened, this earth will be peopled with tsars and lighted up with human glory. Kirilov's pistol shot will be the signal for the last revolution. Thus, it is not despair that urges him to death, but love of his neighbor for his own sake. Before terminating in blood an indescribable spiritual adventure, Kirilov makes a remark as old as human suffering: "All is well."

This theme of suicide in Dostoevsky, then, is indeed an absurd theme. Let us merely note before going on that Kirilov reappears in other characters who themselves set in motion additional absurd themes. Stavrogin and Ivan Karamazov try out the absurd truths in practical life. They are the ones liberated by Kirilov's death. They try their skill at being tsars. Stavrogin leads an

---

[4] "Stavrogin: 'Do you believe in eternal life in the other world?' Kirilov: 'No, but in eternal life in this world.'"

[5] "Man simply invented God in order not to kill himself. That is the summary of universal history down to this moment."

"ironic" life, and it is well known in what regard. He arouses hatred around him. And yet the key to the character is found in his farewell letter: "I have not been able to detest anything." He is a tsar in indifference. Ivan is likewise by refusing to surrender the royal powers of the mind. To those who, like his brother, prove by their lives that it is essential to humiliate one-self in order to believe, he might reply that the condition is shameful. His key word is: "Everything is permitted," with the appropriate shade of melancholy. Of course, like Nietzsche, the most famous of God's assassins, he ends in madness. But this is a risk worth running, and, faced with such tragic ends, the essential impulse of the absurd mind is to ask: "What does that prove?"

Thus the novels, like the *Diary*, propound the absurd question. They establish logic unto death, exaltation, "dreadful" freedom, the glory of the tsars become human. All is well, everything is permitted, and nothing is hateful—these are absurd judgments. But what an amazing creation in which those creatures of fire and ice seem so familiar to us. The passionate world of indifference that rumbles in their hearts does not seem at all monstrous to us. We recognize in it our everyday anxieties. And probably no one so much as Dostoevsky has managed to give the absurd world such familiar and tormenting charms.

Yet what is his conclusion? Two quotations will show the complete metaphysical reversal that leads the writer to other revelations. The argument of the one who commits logical suicide having provoked protests from the critics, Dostoevsky in the following installments of the *Diary* amplifies his position and concludes thus: "If faith in immortality is so necessary to the human being (that without it he comes to the point of killing himself), it must therefore be the normal state of humanity. Since this is the case, the immortality of the human soul exists without any doubt." Then again in the last pages of his last novel, at the conclusion of that gigantic combat with God, some children ask Aliocha: "Karamazov, is it true what religion says, that we shall rise from the dead, that we shall see one another again?" And Aliocha answers: "Certainly, we shall see one another again, we shall joyfully tell one another everything that has happened."

Thus Kirilov, Stavrogin, and Ivan are defeated. *The Brothers Karamazov* replies to *The Possessed*. And it is indeed a conclusion. Aliocha's case is not ambiguous, as is that of Prince Muichkin. Ill, the latter lives in a perpetual present, tinged with smiles and indifference, and that blissful state might be the eternal life of which the Prince speaks. On the contrary, Aliocha clearly says: "We shall meet again." There is no longer any question of suicide and of madness. What is the use, for anyone who is sure of immortality and of its joys? Man exchanges his divinity for happiness. "We shall joyfully tell one another everything that has happened." Thus again Kirilov's pistol rang out somewhere in Russia, but the world continued to cherish its blind hopes. Men did not understand "that."

Consequently, it is not an absurd novelist addressing us, but an existential novelist. Here, too, the leap is touching and gives its nobility to the art that inspires it. It is a stirring acquiescence, riddled with doubts, uncertain and ardent. Speaking of *The Brothers Karamazov*, Dostoevsky wrote: "The chief question that will be pursued throughout this book is the very one from which I have suffered consciously or unconsciously all life long: the existence of God." It is hard to believe that a novel sufficed to transform into joyful certainty the suffering of a lifetime. One commentator[6] correctly pointed out that Dostoevsky is on Ivan's side and that the affirmative chapters took three months of effort whereas what he called "the blasphemies" were written in three weeks in a state of excitement. There is not one of his characters who does not have that thorn in the flesh, who does not aggravate it or seek a remedy for it in sensation or immortality.[7] In any case, let us remain with this doubt. Here is a work which, in a chiaroscuro more gripping than the light of day, permits us to seize man's struggle against

---

[6] Boris de Schloezer.

[7] Gide's curious and penetrating remark: almost all Dostoevsky's heroes are polygamous.

his hopes. Having reached the end, the creator makes his choice against his characters. That contradiction thus allows us to make a distinction. It is not an absurd work that is involved here, but a work that propounds the absurd problem.

Dostoevsky's reply is humiliation, "shame" according to Stavrogin. An absurd work, on the contrary, does not provide a reply; that is the whole difference. Let us note this carefully in conclusion: what contradicts the absurd in that work is not its Christian character, but rather its announcing a future life. It is possible to be Christian and absurd. There are examples of Christians who do not believe in a future life. In regard to the work of art, it should therefore be possible to define one of the directions of the absurd analysis that could have been anticipated in the preceding pages. It leads to propounding "the absurdity of the Gospel." It throws light upon this idea, fertile in repercussions, that convictions do not prevent incredulity. On the contrary, it is easy to see that the author of *The Possessed*, familiar with these paths, in conclusion took a quite different way. The surprising reply of the creator to his characters, of Dostoevsky to Kirilov, can indeed be summed up thus: existence is illusory *and* it is eternal.

Ephemeral Creation

At this point I perceive, therefore, that hope cannot be eluded forever and that it can beset even those who wanted to be free of it. This is the interest I find in the works discussed up to this point. I could, at least in the realm of creation, list some truly absurd works.[8] But everything must have a beginning. The object of this quest is a certain fidelity. The Church has been so harsh with heretics only because she deemed that there is no worse enemy than a child who has gone astray. But the record of Gnostic effronteries and the persistence of Manichean currents have contributed more to the construction of orthodox dogma than all the prayers. With due allowance, the same is true of the absurd. One recognizes one's course by discovering the paths that

[8] Melville's *Moby Dick*, for instance.

stray from it. At the very conclusion of the absurd reasoning, in one of the attitudes dictated by its logic, it is not a matter of indifference to find hope coming back in under one of its most touching guises. That shows the difficulty of the absurd *ascesis*. Above all, it shows the necessity of unfailing alertness and thus confirms the general plan of this essay.

But if it is still too early to list absurd works, at least a conclusion can be reached as to the creative attitude, one of those which can complete absurd existence. Art can never be so well served as by a negative thought. Its dark and humiliated proceedings are as necessary to the understanding of a great work as black is to white. To work and create "for nothing," to sculpture in clay, to know that one's creation has no future, to see one's work destroyed in a day while being aware that fundamentally this has no more importance than building for centuries—this is the difficult wisdom that absurd thought sanctions. Performing these two tasks simultaneously, negating on the one hand and magnifying on the other, is the way open to the absurd creator. He must give the void its colors.

This leads to a special conception of the work of art. Too often the work of a creator is looked upon as a series of isolated testimonies. Thus, artist and man of letters are confused. A profound thought is in a constant state of becoming; it adopts the experience of a life and assumes its shape. Likewise, a man's sole creation is strengthened in its successive and multiple aspects: his works. One after another, they complement one another, correct or overtake one another, contradict one another too. If something brings creation to an end, it is not the victorious and illusory cry of the blinded artist: "I have said everything," but the death of the creator which closes his experience and the book of his genius.

That effort, that superhuman consciousness are not necessarily apparent to the reader. There is no mystery in human creation. Will performs this miracle. But at least there is no true creation without a secret. To be sure, a succession of works can be but a series of approximations of the same thought. But it is possible to conceive of another type of creator proceeding by juxta-

position. Their works may seem to be devoid of inter-
relations. To a certain degree, they are contradictory.
But viewed all together, they resume their natural grouping. From death, for instance, they derive their definitive significance. They receive their most obvious light
from the very life of their author. At the moment of
death, the succession of his works is but a collection of
failures. But if those failures all have the same resonance, the creator has managed to repeat the image of
his own condition, to make the air echo with the sterile
secret he possesses.

The effort to dominate is considerable here. But human intelligence is up to much more. It will merely in-
dicate clearly the voluntary aspect of creation. Elsewhere I have brought out the fact that human will had
no other purpose than to maintain awareness. But that
could not do without discipline. Of all the schools of
patience and lucidity, creation is the most effective. It
is also the staggering evidence of man's sole dignity: the
dogged revolt against his condition, perseverance in an
effort considered sterile. It calls for a daily effort, self-
mastery, a precise estimate of the limits of truth, measure, and strength. It constitutes an *ascesis*. All that "for
nothing," in order to repeat and mark time. But perhaps
the great work of art has less importance in itself than
in the ordeal it demands of a man and the opportunity
it provides him of overcoming his phantoms and ap-
proaching a little closer to his naked reality.

Let there be no mistake in æsthetics. It is not patient
inquiry, the unceasing, sterile illustration of a thesis that
I am calling for here. Quite the contrary, if I have made
myself clearly understood. The thesis-novel, the work
that proves, the most hateful of all, is the one that most
often is inspired by a *smug* thought. You demonstrate
the truth you feel sure of possessing. But those are ideas
one launches, and ideas are the contrary of thought.
Those creators are philosophers, ashamed of themselves.
Those I am speaking of or whom I imagine are, on the
contrary, lucid thinkers. At a certain point where thought
turns back on itself, they raise up the images of their

works like the obvious symbols of a limited, mortal, and rebellious thought.

They perhaps prove something. But those proofs are ones that the novelists provide for themselves rather than for the world in general. The essential is that the novelists should triumph in the concrete and that this constitute their nobility. This wholly carnal triumph has been prepared for them by a thought in which abstract powers have been humiliated. When they are completely so, at the same time the flesh makes the creation shine forth in all its absurd luster. After all, ironic philosophies produce passionate works.

Any thought that abandons unity glorifies diversity. And diversity is the home of art. The only thought to liberate the mind is that which leaves it alone, certain of its limits and of its impending end. No doctrine tempts it. It awaits the ripening of the work and of life. Detached from it, the work will once more give a barely muffled voice to a soul forever freed from hope. Or it will give voice to nothing if the creator, tired of his activity, intends to turn away. That is equivalent.

Thus, I ask of absurd creation what I required from thought—revolt, freedom, and diversity. Later on it will manifest its utter futility. In that daily effort in which intelligence and passion mingle and delight each other, the absurd man discovers a discipline that will make up the greatest of his strengths. The required diligence, the doggedness and lucidity thus resemble the conqueror's attitude. To create is likewise to give a shape to one's fate. For all these characters, their work defines them at least as much as it is defined by them. The actor taught us this: there is no frontier between being and appearing.

Let me repeat. None of all this has any real meaning. On the way to that liberty, there is still a progress to be made. The final effort for these related minds, creator or conqueror, is to manage to free themselves also from their undertakings: succeed in granting that the very work, whether it be conquest, love, or creation, may well not be; consummate thus the utter futility of any individual life. Indeed, that gives them more freedom in the realization of that work, just as becoming aware of the absurdity of life authorized them to plunge into it with every excess.

All that remains is a fate whose outcome alone is fatal. Outside of that single fatality of death, everything, joy or happiness, is liberty. A world remains of which man is the sole master. What bound him was the illusion of another world. The outcome of his thought, ceasing to be renunciatory, flowers in images. It frolics —in myths, to be sure, but myths with no other depth than that of human suffering and, like it, inexhaustible. Not the divine fable that amuses and blinds, but the terrestrial face, gesture, and drama in which are summed up a difficult wisdom and an ephemeral passion.

The Myth of Sisyphus

✳

The gods had condemned Sisyphus to ceaselessly rolling a rock to the top of a mountain, whence the stone would fall back of its own weight. They had thought with some reason that there is no more dreadful punishment than futile and hopeless labor.

If one believes Homer, Sisyphus was the wisest and most prudent of mortals. According to another tradition, however, he was disposed to practice the profession of highwayman. I see no contradiction in this. Opinions differ as to the reasons why he became the futile laborer of the underworld. To begin with, he is accused of a certain levity in regard to the gods. He stole their secrets. Ægina, the daughter of Æsopus, was carried off by Jupiter. The father was shocked by that disappearance and complained to Sisyphus. He, who knew of the abduction, offered to tell about it on condition that Æsopus would give water to the citadel of Corinth. To the celestial thunderbolts he preferred the benediction of water. He was punished for this in the underworld. Homer tells us also that Sisyphus had put Death in chains. Pluto could not endure the sight of his deserted, silent empire. He dispatched the god of war, who liberated Death from the hands of her conqueror.

It is said also that Sisyphus, being near to death, rashly wanted to test his wife's love. He ordered her to cast his unburied body into the middle of the public square. Sisyphus woke up in the underworld. And there, annoyed by an obedience so contrary to human love, he obtained from Pluto permission to return to earth in order to chastise his wife. But when he had seen again the face of this world, enjoyed water and sun, warm stones and the sea, he no longer wanted to go back to the infernal darkness. Recalls, signs of anger, warnings were of no avail. Many years more he lived facing the curve of the gulf, the sparkling sea, and the smiles of earth. A decree of the gods was necessary. Mercury came and seized the impudent man by the collar and, snatching him from his joys, led him forcibly back to the underworld, where his rock was ready for him.

You have already grasped that Sisyphus is the absurd hero. He *is*, as much through his passions as through his torture. His scorn of the gods, his hatred of death, and his passion for life won him that unspeakable penalty in which the whole being is exerted toward accomplishing nothing. This is the price that must be paid for the passions of this earth. Nothing is told us about Sisyphus in the underworld. Myths are made for the imagination to breathe life into them. As for this myth, one sees merely the whole effort of a body straining to raise the huge stone, to roll it and push it up a slope a hundred times over; one sees the face screwed up, the cheek tight against the stone, the shoulder bracing the clay-covered mass, the foot wedging it, the fresh start with arms outstretched, the wholly human security of two earth-clotted hands. At the very end of his long effort measured by skyless space and time without depth, the purpose is achieved. Then Sisyphus watches the stone rush down in a few moments toward that lower world whence he will have to push it up again toward the summit. He goes back down to the plain.

It is during that return, that pause, that Sisyphus interests me. A face that toils so close to stones is already stone itself! I see that man going back down with a heavy yet measured step toward the torment of which he will never know the end. That hour like a breathing-space which returns as surely as his suffering, that is the hour of consciousness. At each of those moments when he leaves the heights and gradually sinks toward the lairs of the gods, he is superior to his fate. He is stronger than his rock.

If this myth is tragic, that is because its hero is conscious. Where would his torture be, indeed, if at every step the hope of succeeding upheld him? The workman of today works every day in his life at the same tasks, and this fate is no less absurd. But it is tragic only at the rare moments when it becomes conscious. Sisyphus, proletarian of the gods, powerless and rebellious, knows the whole extent of his wretched condition: it is what he thinks of during his descent. The lucidity that was to constitute his torture at the same time crowns his victory. There is no fate that cannot be surmounted by scorn.

If the descent is thus sometimes performed in sorrow, it can also take place in joy. This word is not too much. Again I fancy Sisyphus returning toward his rock, and the sorrow was in the beginning. When the images of earth cling too tightly to memory, when the call of happiness becomes too insistent, it happens that melancholy rises in man's heart: this is the rock's victory, this is the rock itself. The boundless grief is too heavy to bear. These are our nights of Gethsemane. But crushing truths perish from being acknowledged. Thus, Œdipus at the outset obeys fate without knowing it. But from the moment he knows, his tragedy begins. Yet at the same moment, blind and desperate, he realizes that the only bond linking him to the world is the cool hand of a girl. Then a tremendous remark rings out: "Despite so many ordeals, my advanced age and the nobility of my soul make me conclude that all is well." Sophocles' Œdipus, like Dostoevsky's Kirilov, thus gives the recipe for the absurd victory. Ancient wisdom confirms modern heroism.

One does not discover the absurd without being tempted to write a manual of happiness. "What! by such narrow ways—?" There is but one world, however. Happiness and the absurd are two sons of the same earth. They are inseparable. It would be a mistake to say that happiness necessarily springs from the absurd discovery. It happens as well that the feeling of the absurd springs from happiness. "I conclude that all is well," says Œdipus, and that remark is sacred. It echoes in the wild and limited universe of man. It teaches that all is not, has not been, exhausted. It drives out of this world a god who had come into it with dissatisfaction and a preference for futile sufferings. It makes of fate a human matter, which must be settled among men.

All Sisyphus' silent joy is contained therein. His fate belongs to him. His rock is his thing. Likewise, the absurd man, when he contemplates his torment, silences all the idols. In the universe suddenly restored to its silence, the myriad wondering little voices of the earth rise up. Unconscious, secret calls, invitations from all the faces, they are the necessary reverse and price of victory. There is no sun without shadow, and it is essential to know the night. The absurd man says yes and his effort will henceforth be unceasing. If there is a personal fate, there is no higher destiny, or at least there is but one which he concludes is inevitable and despicable. For the rest, he knows himself to be the master of his days. At that subtle moment when man glances backward over his life, Sisyphus returning toward his rock, in that slight pivoting he contemplates that series of unrelated actions which becomes his fate, created by him, combined under his memory's eye and soon sealed by his death. Thus, convinced of the wholly human origin of all that is human, a blind man eager to see who knows that the night has no end, he is still on the go. The rock is still rolling.

I leave Sisyphus at the foot of the mountain! One always finds one's burden again. But Sisyphus teaches the higher fidelity that negates the gods and raises rocks. He too concludes that all is well. This universe henceforth without a master seems to him neither sterile nor futile. Each atom of that stone, each mineral flake of that night-filled mountain, in itself forms a world. The struggle itself toward the heights is enough to fill a man's heart. One must imagine Sisyphus happy.

Appendix

*

Hope and the Absurd in the Work of Franz Kafka

The whole art of Kafka consists in forcing the reader to reread. His endings, or his absence of endings, suggest explanations which, however, are not revealed in clear language but, before they seem justified, require that the story be reread from another point of view. Sometimes there is a double possibility of interpretation, whence appears the necessity for two readings. This is what the author wanted. But it would be wrong to try to interpret everything in Kafka in detail. A symbol is always in general and, however precise its translation, an artist can restore to it only its movement: there is no word-for-word rendering. Moreover, nothing is harder to understand than a symbolic work. A symbol always transcends the one who makes use of it and makes him say in reality more than he is aware of expressing. In this regard, the surest means of getting hold of it is not to provoke it, to begin the work without a preconceived attitude and not to look for its hidden currents. For Kafka in particular it is fair to agree to his rules, to approach the drama through its externals and the novel through its form.

At first glance and for a casual reader, they are disturbing adventures that carry off quaking and dogged characters into pursuit of problems they never formulate. In *The Trial*, Joseph K. is accused. But he doesn't know of what. He is doubtless eager to defend himself, but he doesn't know why. The lawyers find his case difficult. Meanwhile, he does not neglect to love, to eat, or to read his paper. Then he is judged. But the courtroom is very dark. He doesn't understand much. He merely assumes that he is condemned, but to what he barely wonders. At times he suspects just the same, and he continues living. Some time later two well-dressed and polite gentlemen come to get him and invite him to follow them. Most courteously they lead him into a wretched suburb, put his head on a stone, and slit his throat. Before dying the condemned man says merely: "Like a dog."

You see that it is hard to speak of a symbol in a tale whose most obvious quality just happens to be naturalness. But naturalness is a hard category to understand. There are works in which the event seems natural to the reader. But there are others (rarer, to be sure) in which the character considers natural what happens to him. By an odd but obvious paradox, the more extraordinary the character's adventures are, the more noticeable will be the naturalness of the story: it is in proportion to the divergence we feel between the strangeness of a man's life and the simplicity with which that man accepts it. It seems that this naturalness is Kafka's. And, precisely, one is well aware what *The Trial* means. People have spoken of an image of the human condition. To be sure. Yet it is both simpler and more complex. I mean that the significance of the novel is more particular and more personal to Kafka. To a certain degree, he is the one who does the talking, even though it is me he confesses. He lives and he is condemned. He learns this on the first pages of the novel he is pursuing in this world, and if he tries to cope with this, he nonetheless does so without surprise. He will never show sufficient astonishment at this lack of astonishment. It is by such contradictions that the first signs of the absurd work are recognized. The mind projects into the concrete its spiritual tragedy. And it can do so solely by means of a perpetual paradox which confers on colors the power to express the void and on daily gestures the strength to translate eternal ambitions.

Likewise, *The Castle* is perhaps a theology in action, but it is first of all the individual adventure of a soul in quest of its grace, of a man who asks of this world's objects their royal secret and of women the signs of the god that sleeps in them. *Metamorphosis*, in turn, certainly represents the horrible imagery of an ethic of lucidity. But it is also the product of that incalculable amazement man feels at being conscious of the beast he becomes effortlessly. In this fundamental ambiguity lies Kafka's secret. These perpetual oscillations between the natural and the extraordinary, the individual and the universal, the tragic and the everyday, the absurd and the logical, are found throughout his work and give it both its resonance and its meaning. These are the paradoxes that must be enumerated, the contradictions that must be strengthened, in order to understand the absurd work.

A symbol, indeed, assumes two planes, two worlds of ideas and sensations, and a dictionary of correspondences between them. This lexicon is the hardest thing to draw up. But awaking to the two worlds brought face to face is tantamount to getting on the trail of their secret relationships. In Kafka these two worlds are that of everyday life on the one hand and, on the other, that of supernatural anxiety.[1] It seems that we are witnessing here an interminable exploitation of Nietzsche's remark: "Great problems are in the street."

There is in the human condition (and this is a commonplace of all literatures) a basic absurdity as well as an implacable nobility. The two coincide, as is natural. Both of them are represented, let me repeat, in the ridiculous divorce separating our spiritual excesses and the ephemeral joys of the body. The absurd thing is that it should be the soul of this body which it transcends so inordinately. Whoever would like to represent this absurdity must give it life in a series of parallel contrasts. Thus it is that Kafka expresses tragedy by the everyday and the absurd by the logical.

[1] It is worth noting that the works of Kafka can quite as legitimately be interpreted in the sense of a social criticism (for instance in *The Trial*). It is probable, moreover, that there is no need to choose. Both interpretations are good. In absurd terms, as we have seen, revolt against men is also directed against God: great revolutions are always metaphysical.

An actor lends more force to a tragic character the more careful he is not to exaggerate it. If he is moderate, the horror he inspires will be immoderate. In this regard Greek tragedy is rich in lessons. In a tragic work fate always makes itself felt better in the guise of logic and naturalness. Œdipus's fate is announced in advance. It is decided supernaturally that he will commit the murder and the incest. The drama's whole effort is to show the logical system which, from deduction to deduction, will crown the hero's misfortune. Merely to announce to us that uncommon fate is scarcely horrible, because it is improbable. But if its necessity is demonstrated to us in the framework of everyday life, society, state, familiar emotion, then the horror is hallowed. In that revolt that shakes man and makes him say: "That is not possible," there is an element of desperate certainty that "that" can be.

This is the whole secret of Greek tragedy, or at least of one of its aspects. For there is another which, by a reverse method, would help us to understand Kafka better. The human heart has a tiresome tendency to label as fate only what crushes it. But happiness likewise, in its way, is without reason, since it is inevitable. Modern man, however, takes the credit for it himself, when he doesn't fail to recognize it. Much could be said, on the contrary, about the privileged fates of Greek tragedy and those favored in legend who, like Ulysses, in the midst of the worst adventures are saved from themselves. It was not so easy to return to Ithaca.

What must be remembered in any case is that secret complicity that joins the logical and the everyday to the tragic. This is why Samsa, the hero of *Metamorphosis*, is a traveling salesman. This is why the only thing that disturbs him in the strange adventure that makes a vermin of him is that his boss will be angry at his absence. Legs and feelers grow out on him, his spine arches up, white spots appear on his belly and—I shall not say that this does not astonish him, for the effect would be spoiled—but it causes him a "slight annoyance." The whole art of Kafka is in that distinction. In his central work, *The Castle*, the details of everyday life stand out, and yet in that strange novel in which nothing concludes and everything begins over again, it is the essential adventure of a soul in quest of its grace that is represented. That translation of the problem into action, that coincidence of the general and the particular are recognized likewise in the little artifices that belong to every great creator. In *The Trial* the hero might have been named Schmidt or Franz Kafka. But he is named Joseph K. He is not Kafka and yet he is Kafka. He is an average European. He is like everybody else. But he is also the entity K. who is the *x* of this flesh-and-blood equation.

Likewise, if Kafka wants to express the absurd, he will make use of consistency. You know the story of the crazy man who was fishing in a bathtub. A doctor with ideas as to psychiatric treatments asked him "if they were biting," to which he received the harsh reply: "Of course not, you fool, since this is a bathtub." That story belongs to the baroque type. But in it can be grasped quite clearly to what a degree the absurd effect is linked to an excess of logic. Kafka's world is in truth an indescribable universe in which man allows himself the tormenting luxury of fishing in a bathtub, knowing that nothing will come of it.

Consequently, I recognize here a work that is absurd in its principles. As for *The Trial*, for instance, I can indeed say that it is a complete success. Flesh wins out. Nothing is lacking, neither the unexpressed revolt (but *it* is what is writing), nor lucid and mute despair (but *it* is what is creating), nor that amazing freedom of manner which the characters of the novel exemplify until their ultimate death.

Yet this world is not so closed as it seems. Into this universe devoid of progress, Kafka is going to introduce hope in a strange form. In this regard *The Trial* and *The Castle* do not follow the same direction. They complement each other. The barely perceptible progression from one to the other represents a tremendous conquest in the realm of evasion. *The Trial* propounds a problem which *The Castle*, to a certain degree, solves. The first describes according to a quasi-scientific method and without concluding. The second, to a certain degree, explains. *The Trial* diagnoses, and *The Castle* imagines a treatment. But the remedy proposed here does not cure. It merely brings the malady back into normal life. It helps to accept it. In a certain sense (let us think of Kierkegaard), it makes people cherish it. The Land Surveyor K. cannot imagine another anxiety than the one that is tormenting him. The very people around him become attached to that void and that nameless pain, as if suffering assumed in this case a privileged aspect. "How I need you," Frieda says to K. "How forsaken I feel, since knowing you, when you are not with me." This subtle remedy that makes us love what crushes us and makes hope spring up in a world without issue, this sudden "leap" through which everything is changed, is the secret of the existential revolution and of *The Castle* itself.

Few works are more rigorous in their development than *The Castle*. K. is named Land Surveyor to the Castle and he arrives in the village. But from the village to the Castle it is impossible to communicate. For hundreds of pages K. persists in seeking his way, makes every advance, uses trickery and expedients, never gets angry, and with disconcerting good will tries to assume the duties entrusted to him. Each chapter is a new frustration. And also a new beginning. It is not logic, but consistent method. The scope of that insistence constitutes the work's tragic quality. When K. telephones to the Castle, he hears confused, mingled voices, vague laughs, distant invitations. That is enough to feed his hope, like those few signs appearing in summer skies or those evening anticipations which make up our reason for living. Here is found the secret of the melancholy peculiar to Kafka. The same, in truth, that is found in Proust's work or in the landscape of Plotinus: a nostalgia for a lost paradise. "I become very sad," says Olga, "when Barnabas tells me in the morning that he is going to the Castle: that probably futile trip, that probably wasted day, that probably empty hope." "Probably"—on this implication Kafka gambles his entire work. But nothing avails; the quest of the eternal here is meticulous. And those inspired automata, Kafka's characters, provide us with a precise image of what we should be if we were deprived of our distractions[2] and utterly consigned to the humiliations of the divine.

In *The Castle* that surrender to the everyday becomes an ethic. The great hope of K. is to get the Castle to adopt him. Unable to achieve this alone, his whole effort is to deserve this favor by becoming an inhabitant of the village, by losing the status of foreigner that everyone makes him feel. What he wants is an occupation, a home, the life of a healthy, normal man. He can't stand his madness any longer. He wants to be reasonable. He wants to cast off the peculiar curse that makes him a stranger to the village. The episode of Frieda is significant in this regard. If he takes as his mistress this woman who has known one of the Castle's officials, this is because of her past. He derives from her something that transcends him—while being aware of what makes her forever unworthy of the Castle. This makes one think of Kierkegaard's strange love for Regina Olsen. In certain men, the fire of eternity consuming them is great enough for them to burn in it the very heart of those closest to them. The fatal mistake that consists in giving to God what is not God's is likewise the subject of this episode of *The Castle*. But for Kafka it seems that this is not a mistake. It is a doctrine and a "leap." There is nothing that is not God's.

Even more significant is the fact that the Land Surveyor breaks with Frieda in order to go toward the Barnabas sisters. For the Barnabas family is the only one in the village that is utterly forsaken by the Castle and by the village itself. Amalia, the elder sister, has rejected the shameful propositions made her by one of the Castle's officials. The immoral curse that followed has forever cast her out from the love of God. Being incapable of losing one's honor for God amounts to making oneself unworthy of his grace. You recognize a theme familiar to existential philosophy: truth contrary to

[2] In *The Castle* it seems that "distractions" in the Pascalian sense are represented by the assistants who "distract" K. from his anxiety. If Frieda eventually becomes the mistress of one of the assistants, this is because she prefers the stage setting to truth, everyday life to shared anguish.

morality. At this point things are far-reaching. For the path pursued by Kafka's hero from Frieda to the Barnabas sisters is the very one that leads from trusting love to the deification of the absurd. Here again Kafka's thought runs parallel to Kierkegaard. It is not surprising that the "Barnabas story" is placed at the end of the book. The Land Surveyor's last attempt is to recapture God through what negates him, to recognize him, not according to our categories of goodness and beauty, but behind the empty and hideous aspects of his indifference, of his injustice, and of his hatred. That stranger who asks the Castle to adopt him is at the end of his voyage a little more exiled because this time he is unfaithful to himself, forsaking morality, logic, and intellectual truths in order to try to enter, endowed solely with his mad hope, the desert of divine grace.[3]

The word "hope" used here is not ridiculous. On the contrary, the more tragic the condition described by Kafka, the firmer and more aggressive that hope becomes. The more truly absurd *The Trial* is, the more moving and illegitimate the impassioned "leap" of *The Castle* seems. But we find here again in a pure state the paradox of existential thought as it is expressed, for instance, by Kierkegaard: "Earthly hope must be killed; only then can one be saved by true hope," [4] which can be translated: "One has to have written *The Trial* to undertake *The Castle*."

Most of those who have spoken of Kafka have indeed defined his work as a desperate cry with no recourse left to man. But this calls for review. There is hope and hope. To me the optimistic work of Henri Bordeaux seems peculiarly discouraging. This is because it has nothing for the discriminating. Malraux's thought, on the other hand, is always bracing. But in these two cases neither the same hope nor the same despair is at issue. I see merely that the absurd work itself may lead to the in-

[3] This is obviously true only of the unfinished version of *The Castle* that Kafka left us. But it is doubtful that the writer would have destroyed in the last chapters his novel's unity of tone.

[4] Purity of heart.

fidelity I want to avoid. The work which was but an ineffectual repetition of a sterile condition, a lucid glorification of the ephemeral, becomes here a cradle of illusions. It explains, it gives a shape to hope. The creator can no longer divorce himself from it. It is not the tragic game it was to be. It gives a meaning to the author's life.

It is strange in any case that works of related inspiration like those of Kafka, Kierkegaard, or Chestov—those, in short, of existential novelists and philosophers completely oriented toward the Absurd and its consequences—should in the long run lead to that tremendous cry of hope.

They embrace the God that consumes them. It is through humility that hope enters in. For the absurd of this existence assures them a little more of supernatural reality. If the course of this life leads to God, there is an outcome after all. And the perseverance, the insistence with which Kierkegaard, Chestov, and Kafka's heroes repeat their itineraries are a special warrant of the uplifting power of that certainty.[5]

Kafka refuses his god moral nobility, evidence, virtue, coherence, but only the better to fall into his arms. The absurd is recognized, accepted, and man is resigned to it, but from then on we know that it has ceased to be the absurd. Within the limits of the human condition, what greater hope than the hope that allows an escape from that condition? As I see once more, existential thought in this regard (and contrary to current opinion) is steeped in a vast hope. The very hope which at the time of early Christianity and the spreading of the good news inflamed the ancient world. But in that leap that characterizes all existential thought, in that insistence, in that surveying of a divinity devoid of surface, how can one fail to see the mark of a lucidity that repudiates itself? It is merely claimed that this is pride abdicating to save itself. Such a repudiation would be fecund. But this does not change that. The moral value of lucidity cannot be diminished in my eyes by calling it sterile like all pride. For a truth also, by its very definition, is sterile. All facts are. In a world where everything is given and nothing is explained,

---

[5] The only character without hope in *The Castle* is Amalia. She is the one with whom the Land Surveyor is most violently contrasted.

the fecundity of a value or of a metaphysic is a notion devoid of meaning.

In any case, you see here in what tradition of thought Kafka's work takes its place. It would indeed be intelligent to consider as inevitable the progression leading from *The Trial* to *The Castle*. Joseph K. and the Land Surveyor K. are merely two poles that attract Kafka.[6] I shall speak like him and say that his work is probably not absurd. But that should not deter us from seeing its nobility and universality. They come from the fact that he managed to represent so fully the everyday passage from hope to grief and from desperate wisdom to intentional blindness. His work is universal (a really absurd work is not universal) to the extent to which it represents the emotionally moving face of man fleeing humanity, deriving from his contradictions reasons for believing, reasons for hoping from his fecund despairs, and calling life his terrifying apprenticeship in death. It is universal because its inspiration is religious. As in all religions, man is freed of the weight of his own life. But if I know that, if I can even admire it, I also know that I am not seeking what is universal, but what is true. The two may well not coincide.

This particular view will be better understood if I say that truly hopeless thought just happens to be defined by the opposite criteria and that the tragic work might be the work that, after all future hope is exiled, describes the life of a happy man. The more exciting life is, the more absurd is the idea of losing it. This is perhaps the secret of that proud aridity felt in Nietzsche's work. In this connection, Nietzsche appears to be the only artist to have derived the extreme consequences of an æsthetic of the Absurd, inasmuch as his final message lies in a sterile and conquering lucidity and an obstinate negation of any supernatural consolation.

The preceding should nevertheless suffice to bring out the capital importance of Kafka in the framework of this essay. Here we are carried to the confines of human

---

[6] On the two aspects of Kafka's thought, compare "In the Penal Colony," published by the *Cahiers du Sud* (and in America by *Partisan Review*—translator's note): "Guilt ['of man' is understood] is never doubtful" and a fragment of *The Castle* (Momus's report): "The guilt of the Land Surveyor K. is hard to establish."

thought. In the fullest sense of the word, it can be said that everything in that work is essential. In any case, it propounds the absurd problem altogether. If one wants to compare these conclusions with our initial remarks, the content with the form, the secret meaning of *The Castle* with the natural art in which it is molded, K.'s passionate, proud quest with the everyday setting against which it takes place, then one will realize what may be its greatness. For if nostalgia is the mark of the human, perhaps no one has given such flesh and volume to these phantoms of regret. But at the same time will be sensed what exceptional nobility the absurd work calls for, which is perhaps not found here. If the nature of art is to bind the general to the particular, ephemeral eternity of a drop of water to the play of its lights, it is even truer to judge the greatness of the absurd writer by the distance he is able to introduce between these two worlds. His secret consists in being able to find the exact point where they meet in their greatest disproportion.

And, to tell the truth, this geometrical locus of man and the inhuman is seen everywhere by the pure in heart. If Faust and Don Quixote are eminent creations of art, this is because of the immeasurable nobilities they point out to us with their earthly hands. Yet a moment always comes when the mind negates the truths that those hands can touch. A moment comes when the creation ceases to be taken tragically; it is merely taken seriously. Then man is concerned with hope. But that is not his business. His business is to turn away from subterfuge. Yet this is just what I find at the conclusion of the vehement proceedings Kafka institutes against the whole universe. His unbelievable verdict is this hideous and upsetting world in which the very moles dare to hope.[7]

---

[7] What is offered above is obviously an interpretation of Kafka's work. But it is only fair to add that nothing prevents its being considered, aside from any interpretation, from a purely æsthetic point of view. For instance, B. Groethuysen in his remarkable preface to *The Trial* limits himself, more wisely than we, to following merely the painful fancies of what he calls, most strikingly, a daydreamer. It is the fate and perhaps the greatness of that work that it offers everything and confirms nothing.

Other Essays

Summer in Algiers

For Jacques Heurgon

The loves we share with a city are often secret loves. Old walled towns like Paris, Prague, and even Florence are closed in on themselves and hence limit the world that belongs to them. But Algiers (together with certain other privileged places such as cities on the sea) opens to the sky like a mouth or a wound. In Algiers one loves the commonplaces: the sea at the end of every street, a certain volume of sunlight, the beauty of the race. And, as always, in that unashamed offering there is a secret fragrance. In Paris it is possible to be homesick for space and a beating of wings. Here at least man is gratified in every wish and, sure of his desires, can at last measure his possessions.

Probably one has to live in Algiers for some time in order to realize how paralyzing an excess of nature's bounty can be. There is nothing here for whoever would learn, educate himself, or better himself. This country has no lessons to teach. It neither promises nor affords glimpses. It is satisfied to give, but in abundance. It is completely accessible to the eyes, and you know it the moment you enjoy it. Its pleasures are without remedy and its joys without hope. Above all, it requires clairvoyant souls—that is, without solace. It insists upon one's performing an act of lucidity as one performs an act of faith. Strange country that gives the man it nourishes both his splendor and his misery! It is not surprising that the sensual riches granted to a sensitive man of these regions should coincide with the most extreme destitution. No truth fails to carry with it its bitterness. How can one be surprised, then, if I never feel more affection for the face of this country than amid its poorest men?

During their entire youth men find here a life in proportion to their beauty. Then, later on, the downhill slope and obscurity. They wagered on the flesh, but knowing they were to lose. In Algiers whoever is young and alive finds sanctuary and occasion for triumphs everywhere: in the bay, the sun, the red and white games on the seaward terraces, the flowers and sports stadiums, the cool-legged girls. But for whoever has lost his youth there is nothing to cling to and nowhere where melancholy can escape itself. Elsewhere, Italian terraces, European cloisters, or the profile of the Provençal hills—all places where man can flee his humanity and gently liberate himself from himself. But everything here calls for solitude and the blood of young men. Goethe on his deathbed calls for light and this is a historic remark. At Belcourt and Babel-Oued old men seated in the depths of cafés listen to the bragging of young men with plastered hair.

Summer betrays these beginnings and ends to us in Algiers. During those months the city is deserted. But the poor remain, and the sky. We join the former as they go down toward the harbor and man's treasures: warmth of the water and the brown bodies of women. In the evening, sated with such wealth, they return to the oilcloth and kerosene lamp that constitute the whole setting of their life.

In Algiers no one says "go for a swim," but rather "indulge in a swim." The implications are clear. People swim in the harbor and go to rest on the buoys. Anyone who passes near a buoy where a pretty girl already is sunning herself shouts to his friends: "I tell you it's a seagull." These are healthy amusements. They must obviously constitute the ideal of those youths, since most of them continue the same life in the winter, undressing every day at noon for a frugal lunch in the sun. Not that they have read the boring sermons of the nudists, those

Protestants of the flesh (there is a theory of the body quite as tiresome as that of the mind). But they are simply "comfortable in the sunlight." The importance of this custom for our epoch can never be overestimated. For the first time in two thousand years the body has appeared naked on beaches. For twenty centuries men have striven to give decency to Greek insolence and naïveté, to diminish the flesh and complicate dress. Today, despite that history, young men running on Mediterranean beaches repeat the gestures of the athletes of Delos. And living thus among bodies and through one's body, one becomes aware that it has its connotations, its life, and, to risk nonsense, a psychology of its own.[1] The body's evolution, like that of the mind, has its history, its vicissitudes, its progress, and its deficiency. With this distinction, however: color. When you frequent the beach in summer you become aware of a simultaneous progression of all skins from white to golden to tanned, ending up in a tobacco color which marks the extreme limit of the effort of transformation of which the body is capable. Above the harbor stands the set of white cubes of the Kasbah. When you are at water level, against the sharp white background of the Arab town the bodies describe a copper-colored frieze. And as the month of August progresses and the sun grows, the white of the houses becomes more blinding and skins take on a darker warmth. How can one fail to participate, then, in that dialogue of stone and flesh in tune with the sun and seasons? The whole morning has been spent in diving, in bursts of laughter amid splashing water, in vigorous paddles around the red and black freighters (those from Norway with all the scents of wood, those that come from Germany full of the smell of oil, those that go up and down the coast and smell of wine and old casks). At the hour

---

[1] May I take the ridiculous position of saying that I do not like the way Gide exalts the body? He asks it to restrain its desire to make it keener. Thus he comes dangerously near to those who in brothel slang are called involved or brain-workers. Christianity also wants to suspend desire. But, more natural, it sees a mortification in this. My friend Vincent, who is a cooper and junior breast-stroke champion, has an even clearer view. He drinks when he is thirsty, if he desires a woman tries to go to bed with her, and would marry her if he loved her (this hasn't yet happened). Afterward he always says: "I feel better"—and this sums up vigorously any apology that might be made for satiety.

when the sun overflows from every corner of the sky at once, the orange canoe loaded with brown bodies brings us home in a mad race. And when, having suddenly interrupted the cadenced beat of the double paddle's bright-colored wings, we glide slowly in the calm water of the inner harbor, how can I fail to feel that I am piloting through the smooth waters a savage cargo of gods in whom I recognize my brothers?

But at the other end of the city summer is already offering us, by way of contrast, its other riches: I mean its silence and its boredom. That silence is not always of the same quality, depending on whether it springs from the shade or the sunlight. There is the silence of noon on the Place du Gouvernement. In the shade of the trees surrounding it, Arabs sell for five sous glasses of iced lemonade flavored with orange-flowers. Their cry "Cool, cool" can be heard across the empty square. After their cry silence again falls under the burning sun: in the vendor's jug the ice moves and I can hear its tinkle. There is the silence of the siesta. In the streets of the Marine, in front of the dirty barbershops it can be measured in the melodious buzzing of flies behind the hollow reed curtains. Elsewhere, in the Moorish cafés of the Kasbah the body is silent, unable to tear itself away, to leave the glass of tea and rediscover time with the pulsing of its own blood. But, above all, there is the silence of summer evenings.

Those brief moments when day topples into night must be peopled with secret signs and summons for my Algiers to be so closely linked to them. When I spend some time far from that town, I imagine its twilights as promises of happiness. On the hills above the city there are paths among the mastics and olive trees. And toward them my heart turns at such moments. I see flights of black birds rise against the green horizon. In the sky suddenly divested of its sun something relaxes. A whole little nation of red clouds stretches out until it is absorbed in the air. Almost immediately afterward appears the first star that had been seen taking shape and consistency in the depth of the sky. And then suddenly, all consuming, night. What exceptional quality do the fugitive Algerian evenings possess to be able to release so many things in me? I haven't time to tire of that sweetness they leave on my lips before it has disappeared into night. Is this the secret of its persistence? This country's affection is overwhelming and furtive. But during the moment it is present, one's heart at least surrenders completely to it. At Padovani Beach the dance hall is open every day. And in that huge rectangular box with its entire side open to the sea, the poor young people of the neighborhood dance until evening. Often I used to await there a moment of exceptional beauty. During the day the hall is protected by sloping wooden awnings. When the sun goes down they are raised. Then the hall is filled with an odd green light born of the double shell of the sky and the sea. When one is seated far from the windows, one sees only the sky and, silhouetted against it, the faces of the dancers passing in succession. Sometimes a waltz is being played, and against the green background the black profiles whirl obstinately like those cut-out silhouettes that are attached to a phonograph's turntable. Night comes rapidly after this, and with it the lights. But I am unable to relate the thrill and secrecy that subtle instant holds for me. I recall at least a magnificent tall girl who had danced all afternoon. She was wearing a jasmine garland on her tight blue dress, wet with perspiration from the small of her back to her legs. She was laughing as she danced and throwing back her head. As she passed the tables, she left behind her a mingled scent of flowers and flesh. When evening came, I could no longer see her body pressed tight to her partner, but against the sky whirled alternating spots of white jasmine and black hair, and when she would throw back her swelling breast I would hear her laugh and see her partner's profile suddenly plunge forward. I owe to such evenings the idea I have of innocence. In any case, I learn not to separate these creatures bursting with violent energy from the sky where their desires whirl.

In the neighborhood movies in Algiers peppermint lozenges are sometimes sold with, stamped in red, all that is necessary to the awakening of love: (1) questions: "When will you marry me?" "Do you love me?" and

(2) replies: "Madly," "Next spring." After having prepared the way, you pass them to your neighbor, who answers likewise or else turns a deaf ear. At Belcourt marriages have been arranged this way and whole lives been pledged by the mere exchange of peppermint lozenges. And this really depicts the childlike people of this region.

The distinguishing mark of youth is perhaps a magnificent vocation for facile joys. But, above all, it is a haste to live that borders on waste. At Belcourt, as at Bab-el-Oued, people get married young. They go to work early and in ten years exhaust the experience of a lifetime. A thirty-year-old workman has already played all the cards in his hand. He awaits the end between his wife and his children. His joys have been sudden and merciless, as has been his life. One realizes that he is born of this country where everything is given to be taken away. In that plenty and profusion life follows the sweep of great passions, sudden, exacting, and generous. It is not to be built up, but to be burned up. Stopping to think and becoming better are out of the question. The notion of hell, for instance, is merely a funny joke here. Such imaginings are allowed only to the very virtuous. And I really think that virtue is a meaningless word in all Algeria. Not that these men lack principles. They have their code, and a very special one. You are not disrespectful to your mother. You see that your wife is respected in the street. You show consideration for a pregnant woman. You don't double up on an adversary, because "that looks bad." Whoever does not observe these elementary commandments "is not a man," and the question is decided. This strikes me as fair and strong. There are still many of us who automatically observe this code of the street, the only disinterested one I know. But at the same time the shopkeeper's ethics are unknown. I have always seen faces around me filled with pity at the sight of a man between two policemen. And before knowing whether the man had stolen, killed his father, or was merely a nonconformist, they would say: "The poor fellow," or else, with a hint of admiration: "He's a pirate, all right."

There are races born for pride and life. They are the ones that nourish the strangest vocation for boredom. It is also among them that the attitude toward death is the most repulsive. Aside from sensual pleasure, the amusements of this race are among the silliest. A society of bowlers and association banquets, the three-franc movies and parish feasts have for years provided the recreation of those over thirty. Algiers Sundays are among the most sinister. How, then, could this race devoid of spirituality clothe in myths the profound horror of its life? Everything related to death is either ridiculous or hateful here. This populace without religion and without idols dies alone after having lived in a crowd. I know no more hideous spot than the cemetery on Boulevard Bru, opposite one of the most beautiful landscapes in the world. An accumulation of bad taste among the black fencings allows a dreadful melancholy to rise from this spot where death shows her true likeness. "Everything fades," say the heart-shaped ex-votos, "except memory." And all insist on that paltry eternity provided us cheaply by the hearts of those who loved us. The same words fit all despairs. Addressed to the dead man, they speak to him in the second person (our memory will never forsake you); lugubrious pretense which attributes a body and desires to what is at best a black liquid. Elsewhere, amid a deadly profusion of marble flowers and birds, this bold assertion: "Never will your grave be without flowers." But never fear: the inscription surrounds a gilded stucco bouquet, very time-saving for the living (like those immortelles which owe their pompous name to the gratitude of those who still jump onto moving buses). Inasmuch as it is essential to keep up with the times, the classic warbler is sometimes replaced by an astounding pearl airplane piloted by a silly angel who, without regard for logic, is provided with an impressive pair of wings.

Yet how to bring out that these images of death are never separated from life? Here the values are closely linked. The favorite joke of Algerian undertakers, when driving an empty hearse, is to shout: "Want a ride, sister?" to any pretty girls they meet on the way. There is no objection to seeing a symbol in this, even if somewhat untoward. It may seem blasphemous, likewise, to reply to the announcement of a death while winking one's left eye: "Poor fellow, he'll never sing again," or, like that woman of Oran who had never loved her husband: "God gave him to me and God has taken him from me." But, all in all, I see nothing sacred in death and am well aware, on the other hand, of the distance there is between fear and respect. Everything here suggests the horror of dying in a country that invites one to live. And yet it is under the very walls of this cemetery that the young of Belcourt have their assignations and that the girls offer themselves to kisses and caresses.

I am well aware that such a race cannot be accepted by all. Here intelligence has no place as in Italy. This race is indifferent to the mind. It has a cult for and admiration of the body. Whence its strength, its innocent cynicism, and a puerile vanity which explains why it is so severely judged. It is commonly blamed for its "mentality"—that is, a way of seeing and of living. And it is true that a certain intensity of life is inseparable from injustice. Yet here is a race without past, without tradition, and yet not without poetry—but a poetry whose quality I know well, harsh, carnal, far from tenderness, that of their very sky, the only one in truth to move me and bring me inner peace. The contrary of a civilized nation is a creative nation. I have the mad hope that, without knowing it perhaps, these barbarians lounging on beaches are actually modeling the image of a culture in which the greatness of man will at last find its true likeness. This race, wholly cast into its present, lives without myths, without solace. It has put all its possessions on this earth and therefore remains without defense against death. All the gifts of physical beauty have been lavished on it. And with them, the strange avidity that always accompanies that wealth without future. Everything that is done here shows a horror of stability and a disregard for the future. People are in haste to live, and if an art were to be born here it would obey that hatred of permanence that made the Dorians fashion their first column in wood. And yet, yes, one can find measure as well as excess in the violent and keen face of this race, in this summer sky with nothing tender in it, before which all truths can be uttered and on which no deceptive divinity has traced the signs of hope or of redemption. Between this sky and these faces turned toward it, nothing on which to hang a mythology, a literature, an ethic, or a religion, but stones, flesh, stars, and those truths the hand can touch.

To feel one's attachment to a certain region, one's love for a certain group of men, to know that there is always a spot where one's heart will feel at peace—these are many certainties for a single human life. And yet this is not enough. But at certain moments everything yearns for that spiritual home. "Yes, we must go back there—there, indeed." Is there anything odd in finding on earth that union that Plotinus longed for? Unity is expressed here in terms of sun and sea. The heart is sensitive to it through a certain savor of flesh which constitutes its bitterness and its grandeur. I learn that there is no superhuman happiness, no eternity outside the sweep of days. These paltry and essential belongings, these relative truths are the only ones to stir me. As for the others, the "ideal" truths, I have not enough soul to understand them. Not that one must be an animal, but I find no meaning in the happiness of angels. I know simply that this sky will last longer than I. And what shall I call eternity except what will continue after my death? I am not expressing here the creature's satisfaction with his condition. It is quite a different matter. It is not always easy to be a man, still less to be a pure man. But being pure is recovering that spiritual home where one can feel the world's relationship, where one's pulsebeats coincide with the violent throbbing of the two-o'clock sun. It is well known that one's native land is always recognized at the moment of losing it. For those who are too uneasy about themselves, their native land is the one that negates them. I should not like to be brutal or seem extravagant. But, after all, what negates me in this life is first of all what kills me. Everything that exalts life at the same time increases its absurdity. In the Algerian summer I learn that one thing only is more tragic than suffering, and that is the life of a happy man. But it may be also the way to a greater life because it leads to not cheating.

Many, in fact, feign love of life to evade love itself.

They try their skill at enjoyment and at "indulging in experiences." But this is illusory. It requires a rare vocation to be a sensualist. The life of a man is fulfilled without the aid of his mind, with its backward and forward movements, at one and the same time its solitude and its presences. To see these men of Belcourt working, protecting their wives and children, and often without a reproach, I think one can feel a secret shame. To be sure, I have no illusions about it. There is not much love in the lives I am speaking of. I ought to say that not much remains. But at least they have evaded nothing. There are words I have never really understood, such as "sin." Yet I believe these men have never sinned against life. For if there is a sin against life, it consists perhaps not so much in despairing of life as in hoping for another life and in eluding the implacable grandeur of this life. These men have not cheated. Gods of summer they were at twenty by their enthusiasm for life, and they still are, deprived of all hope. I have seen two of them die. They were full of horror, but silent. It is better thus. From Pandora's box, where all the ills of humanity swarmed, the Greeks drew out hope after all the others, as the most dreadful of all. I know no more stirring symbol; for, contrary to the general belief, hope equals resignation. And to live is not to resign oneself.

This, at least, is the bitter lesson of Algerian summers. But already the season is wavering and summer totters. The first September rains, after such violence and hardening, are like the liberated earth's first tears, as if for a few days this country tried its hand at tenderness. Yet at the same period the carob trees cover all of Algeria with a scent of love. In the evening or after the rain, the whole earth, its womb moist with a seed redolent of bitter almond, rests after having given herself to the sun all summer long. And again that scent hallows the union of man and earth and awakens in us the only really virile love in this world: ephemeral and noble.

(1936)

The Minotaur

or *The Stop in Oran*

For Pierre Galindo

This essay dates from 1939. The reader will have to bear this in mind to judge of the present-day Oran. Impassioned protests from that beautiful city assure me, as a matter of fact, that all the imperfections have been (or will be) remedied. On the other hand, the beauties extolled in this essay have been jealously respected. Happy and realistic city, Oran has no further need of writers: she is awaiting tourists. (1953)

There are no more deserts. There are no more islands. Yet there is a need for them. In order to understand the world, one has to turn away from it on occasion; in order to serve men better, one has to hold them at a distance for a time. But where can one find the solitude necessary to vigor, the deep breath in which the mind collects itself and courage gauges its strength? There remain big cities. Simply, certain conditions are required.

The cities Europe offers us are too full of the din of the past. A practiced ear can make out the flapping of wings, a fluttering of souls. The giddy whirl of centuries, of revolutions, of fame can be felt there. There one cannot forget that the Occident was forged in a series of uproars. All that does not make for enough silence.

Paris is often a desert for the heart, but at certain moments from the heights of Père-Lachaise there blows a revolutionary wind that suddenly fills that desert with flags and fallen glories. So it is with certain Spanish towns, with Florence or with Prague. Salzburg would be peaceful without Mozart. But from time to time there rings out over the Salzach the great proud cry of Don Juan as he plunges toward hell. Vienna seems more silent; she is a youngster among cities. Her stones are no older than three centuries and their youth is ignorant of melancholy. But Vienna stands at a crossroads of history. Around her echoes the clash of empires. Certain evenings when the sky is suffused with blood, the stone horses on the Ring monuments seem to take wing. In that fleeting moment when everything is reminiscent of power and history, can be distinctly heard, under the charge of the Polish squadrons, the crashing fall of the Ottoman Empire. That does not make for enough silence either.

To be sure, it is just that solitude amid others that men come looking for in European cities. At least, men with a purpose in life. There they can choose their company, take it or leave it. How many minds have been tempered in the trip between their hotel room and the old stones of the Île Saint-Louis! It is true that others have died there of isolation. As for the first, at any rate, there they found their reasons for growing and asserting themselves. They were alone and they weren't alone. Centuries of history and beauty, the ardent testimony of a thousand lives of the past accompanied them along the Seine and spoke to them both of traditions and of conquests. But their youth urged them to invite such company. There comes a time, there come periods, when it is unwelcome. "It's between us two!" exclaims Rastignac, facing the vast mustiness of Paris. Two, yes, but that is still too many!

The desert itself has assumed significance; it has been glutted with poetry. For all the world's sorrows it is a hallowed spot. But at certain moments the heart wants nothing so much as spots devoid of poetry. Descartes, planning to meditate, chose his desert: the most mercantile city of his era. There he found his solitude and the occasion for perhaps the greatest of our virile poems: "The first [precept] was never to accept anything as true unless I knew it to be obviously so." It is possible to have less ambition and the same nostalgia. But during the last three centuries Amsterdam has spawned museums. In order to flee poetry and yet recapture the peace of stones, other deserts are needed, other spots without soul and without reprieve. Oran is one of these.

The Street

I have often heard the people of Oran complain: "There is no interesting circle." No, indeed! You wouldn't want one! A few right-thinking people tried to introduce the customs of another world into this desert, faithful to the principle that it is impossible to advance art or ideas without grouping together.[1] The result is such that the only instructive circles remain those of poker-players, boxing enthusiasts, bowlers, and the local associations. There at least the unsophisticated prevails. After all, there exists a certain nobility that does not lend itself to the lofty. It is sterile by nature. And those who want to find it leave the "circles" and go out into the street.

The streets of Oran are doomed to dust, pebbles, and heat. If it rains, there is a deluge and a sea of mud. But rain or shine, the shops have the same extravagant and absurd look. All the bad taste of Europe and the Orient has managed to converge in them. One finds, helter-skelter, marble greyhounds, ballerinas with swans, versions of Diana the huntress in green galalith, discus-throwers and reapers, everything that is used for birthday and wedding gifts, the whole race of painful figurines constantly called forth by a commercial and playful genie on our mantelpieces. But such perseverance in bad taste takes on a baroque aspect that makes one forgive all. Here, presented in a casket of dust, are the contents of a show

[1] Gogol's Klestakov is met in Oran. He yawns and then: "I feel I shall soon have to be concerned with something lofty."

window: frightful plaster models of deformed feet, a group of Rembrandt drawings "sacrificed at 150 francs each," practical jokes, tricolored wallets, an eighteenth-century pastel, a mechanical donkey made of plush, bottles of Provence water for preserving green olives, and a wretched wooden virgin with an indecent smile. (So that no one can go away ignorant, the "management" has propped at its base a card saying: "Wooden Virgin.")

There can be found in Oran:

1) Cafés with filth-glazed counters sprinkled with the legs and wings of flies, the proprietor always smiling despite his always empty café. A small black coffee used to cost twelve sous and a large one eighteen.

2) Photographers' studios where there has been no progress in technique since the invention of sensitized paper. They exhibit a strange fauna impossible to encounter in the streets, from the pseudo-sailor leaning on a console table to the marriageable girl, badly dressed and arms dangling, standing in front of a sylvan background. It is possible to assume that these are not portraits from life: they are creations.

3) An edifying abundance of funeral establishments. It is not that people die more in Oran than elsewhere, but I fancy merely that more is made of it.

The attractive naïveté of this nation of merchants is displayed even in their advertising. I read, in the handbill of an Oran movie theater, the advertisement for a third-rate film. I note the adjectives "sumptuous," "splendid," "extraordinary," "amazing," "staggering," and "tremendous." At the end the management informs the public of the considerable sacrifices it has undertaken to be able to present this startling "realization." Nevertheless, the price of tickets will not be increased.

It would be wrong to assume that this is merely a manifestation of that love of exaggeration characteristic of the south. Rather, the authors of this marvelous handbill are revealing their sense of psychology. It is essential to overcome the indifference and profound apathy felt in this country the moment there is any question of choosing between two shows, two careers, and, often, even two women. People make up their minds only when forced to do so. And advertising is well aware of this.

It will assume American proportions, having the same reasons, both here and there, for getting desperate.

The streets of Oran inform us as to the two essential pleasures of the local youth: getting one's shoes shined and displaying those same shoes on the boulevard. In order to have a clear idea of the first of these delights, one has to entrust one's shoes, at ten o'clock on a Sunday morning, to the shoe-shiners in Boulevard Galliéni. Perched on high armchairs, one can enjoy that peculiar satisfaction produced, even upon a rank outsider, by the sight of men in love with their job, as the shoe-shiners of Oran obviously are. Everything is worked over in detail. Several brushes, three kinds of cloths, the polish mixed with gasoline. One might think the operation is finished when a perfect shine comes to life under the soft brush. But the same insistent hand covers the glossy surface again with polish, rubs it, dulls it, makes the cream penetrate the heart of the leather, and then brings forth, under the same brush, a double and really definitive gloss sprung from the depths of the leather.

The wonders achieved in this way are then exhibited to the connoisseurs. In order to appreciate such pleasures of the boulevard, you ought to see the masquerade of youth taking place every evening on the main arteries of the city. Between the ages of sixteen and twenty the young people of Oran "Society" borrow their models of elegance from American films and put on their fancy dress before going out to dinner. With wavy, oiled hair protruding from under a felt hat slanted over the left ear and peaked over the right eye, the neck encircled by a collar big enough to accommodate the straggling hair, the microscopic knot of the necktie kept in place by a regulation pin, with thigh-length coat and waist close to the hips, with light-colored and noticeably short trousers, with dazzlingly shiny triple-soled shoes, every evening those youths make the sidewalks ring with their metal-tipped soles. In all things they are bent on imitating the bearing, forthrightness, and superiority of Mr. Clark Gable. For this reason the local carpers commonly nickname those youths, by favor of a casual pronunciation, "Clarques."

At any rate, the main boulevards of Oran are invaded late in the afternoon by an army of attractive adolescents who go to the greatest trouble to look like a bad lot. Inasmuch as the girls of Oran feel traditionally engaged to these softhearted gangsters, they likewise flaunt the make-up and elegance of popular American actresses. Consequently, the same wits call them "Marlenes." Thus on the evening boulevards when the sound of birds rises skyward from the palm trees, dozens of Clarques and Marlenes meet, eye and size up one another, happy to be alive and to cut a figure, indulging for an hour in the intoxication of perfect existences. There can then be witnessed, the jealous say, the meetings of the American Commission. But in these words lies the bitterness of those over thirty who have no connection with such diversions. They fail to appreciate those daily congresses of youth and romance. These are, in truth, the parliaments of birds that are met in Hindu literature. But no one on the boulevards of Oran debates the problem of being or worries about the way to perfection. There remains nothing but flappings of wings, plumed struttings, coquettish and victorious graces, a great burst of carefree song that disappears with the night.

From here I can hear Klestakov: "I shall soon have to be concerned with something lofty." Alas, he is quite capable of it! If he were urged, he would people this desert within a few years. But for the moment a somewhat secret soul must liberate itself in this facile city with its parade of painted girls unable, nevertheless, to simulate emotion, feigning coyness so badly that the pretense is immediately obvious. Be concerned with something lofty! Just see: Santa-Cruz cut out of the rock, the mountains, the flat sea, the violent wind and the sun, the great cranes of the harbor, the trains, the hangars, the quays, and the huge ramps climbing up the city's rock, and in the city itself these diversions and this boredom, this hubbub and this solitude. Perhaps, indeed, all this is not sufficiently lofty. But the great value of such overpopulated islands is that in them the heart strips bare. Silence is no longer possible except in noisy cities. From Amsterdam Descartes writes to the aged Guez de Balzac: "I go out walking every day amid the confusion of a great crowd, with as much freedom and tranquillity as you could do on your garden paths." [2]

The Desert in Oran

Obliged to live facing a wonderful landscape, the people of Oran have overcome this fearful ordeal by covering their city with very ugly constructions. One expects to find a city open to the sea, washed and refreshed by the evening breeze. And aside from the Spanish quarter,[3] one finds a walled town that turns its back to the sea, that has been built up by turning back on itself like a snail. Oran is a great circular yellow wall covered over with a leaden sky. In the beginning you wander in the labyrinth, seeking the sea like the sign of Ariadne. But you turn round and round in pale and oppressive streets, and eventually the Minotaur devours the people of Oran: the Minotaur is boredom. For some time the citizens of Oran have given up wandering. They have accepted being eaten.

It is impossible to know what stone is without coming to Oran. In that dustiest of cities, the pebble is king. It is so much appreciated that shopkeepers exhibit it in their show windows to hold papers in place or even for mere display. Piles of them are set up along the streets, doubtless for the eyes' delight, since a year later the pile is still there. Whatever elsewhere derives its poetry from the vegetable kingdom here takes on a stone face. The hundred or so trees that can be found in the business section have been carefully covered with dust. They are petrified plants whose branches give off an acrid, dusty smell. In Algiers the Arab cemeteries have a well-known mellowness. In Oran, above the Ras-el-Aïn ravine, facing the sea this time, flat against the blue sky, are fields of chalky, friable pebbles in which the sun blinds with its fires. Amid these bare bones of the earth a purple geranium, from time to time, contributes its life and

---

[2] Doubtless in memory of these good words, an Oran lecture-and-discussion group has been founded under the name of *Cogito-Club*.

[3] And the new boulevard called Front-de-Mer.

fresh blood to the landscape. The whole city has solidified in a stony matrix. Seen from Les Planteurs, the depth of the cliffs surrounding it is so great that the landscape becomes unreal, so mineral it is. Man is outlawed from it. So much heavy beauty seems to come from another world.

If the desert can be defined as a soulless place where the sky alone is king, then Oran is awaiting her prophets. All around and above the city the brutal nature of Africa is indeed clad in her burning charms. She bursts the unfortunate stage setting with which she is covered; she shrieks forth between all the houses and over all the roofs. If one climbs one of the roads up the mountain of Santa-Cruz, the first thing to be visible is the scattered colored cubes of Oran. But a little higher and already the jagged cliffs that surround the plateau crouch in the sea like red beasts. Still a little higher and a great vortex of sun and wind sweeps over, airs out, and obscures the untidy city scattered in disorder all over a rocky landscape. The opposition here is between magnificent human anarchy and the permanence of an unchanging sea. This is enough to make a staggering scent of life rise toward the mountainside road.

There is something implacable about the desert. The mineral sky of Oran, her streets and trees in their coating of dust—everything contributes to creating this dense and impassible universe in which the heart and mind are never distracted from themselves, nor from their sole object, which is man. I am speaking here of difficult places of retreat. Books are written on Florence or Athens. Those cities have formed so many European minds that they must have a meaning. They have the means of moving to tears or of uplifting. They quiet a certain spiritual hunger whose bread is memory. But can one be moved by a city where nothing attracts the mind, where the very ugliness is anonymous, where the past is reduced to nothing? Emptiness, boredom, an indifferent sky, what are the charms of such places? Doubtless solitude and, perhaps, the human creature. For a certain race of men, wherever the human creature is beautiful is a bitter native land. Oran is one of its thousand capitals.

Sports

The Central Sporting Club, on rue du Fondouk in Oran, is giving an evening of boxing which it insists will be appreciated by real enthusiasts. Interpreted, this means that the boxers on the bill are far from being stars, that some of them are entering the ring for the first time, and that consequently you can count, if not on the skill, at least on the courage of the opponents. A native having thrilled me with the firm promise that "blood would flow," I find myself that evening among the real enthusiasts.

Apparently the latter never insist on comfort. To be sure, a ring has been set up at the back of a sort of whitewashed garage, covered with corrugated iron and violently lighted. Folding chairs have been lined up in a square around the ropes. These are the "honor rings." Most of the length of the hall has been filled with seats, and behind them opens a large free space called "lounge" by reason of the fact that not one of the five hundred persons in it could take out a handkerchief without causing serious accidents. In this rectangular box live and breathe some thousand men and two or three women—the kind who, according to my neighbor, always insist on "attracting attention." Everybody is sweating fiercely. While waiting for the fights of the "young hopefuls" a gigantic phonograph grinds out a Tino Rossi record. This is the sentimental song before the murder.

The patience of a true enthusiast is unlimited. The fight announced for nine o'clock has not even begun at nine thirty and no one has protested. The spring weather is warm and the smell of a humanity in shirt sleeves is exciting. Lively discussion goes on among the periodic explosions of lemon-soda corks and the tireless lament of the Corsican singer. A few late arrivals are wedged into the audience when a spotlight throws a blinding light onto the ring. The fights of the young hopefuls begin.

The young hopefuls, or beginners, who are fighting for the fun of it, are always eager to prove this by massacring each other at the earliest opportunity, in defiance of technique. They were never able to last more than three rounds. The hero of the evening in this regard is young "Kid Airplane," who in regular life sells lottery tickets on café terraces. His opponent, indeed, hurtled awkwardly out of the ring at the beginning of the second round after contact with a fist wielded like a propeller.

The crowd got somewhat excited, but this is still an act of courtesy. Gravely it breathes in the hallowed air of the embrocation. It watches these series of slow rites and unregulated sacrifices, made even more authentic by the propitiatory designs, on the white wall, of the fighters' shadows. These are the deliberate ceremonial prologues of a savage religion. The trance will not come until later.

And it so happens that the loudspeaker announces Amar, "the tough Oranese who has never disarmed," against Pérez, "the slugger from Algiers." An uninitiate would misinterpret the yelling that greets the introduction of the boxers in the ring. He would imagine some sensational combat in which the boxers were to settle a personal quarrel known to the public. To tell the truth, it *is* a quarrel they are going to settle. But it is the one that for the past hundred years has mortally separated Algiers and Oran. Back in history, these two North African cities would have already bled each other white as Pisa and Florence did in happier times. Their rivalry is all the stronger just because it probably has no basis. Having every reason to like each other, they loathe each other proportionately. The Oranese accuse the citizens of Algiers of "sham." The people of Algiers imply that the Oranese are rustic. These are bloodier insults than they might seem because they are metaphysical. And unable to lay siege to each other, Oran and Algiers meet, compete, and insult each other on the field of sports, statistics, and public works.

Thus a page of history is unfolding in the ring. And the tough Oranese, backed by a thousand yelling voices, is defending against Pérez a way of life and the pride of a province. Truth forces me to admit that Amar is not conducting his discussion well. His argument has a flaw: he lacks reach. The slugger from Algiers, on the contrary, has the required reach in his argument. It lands persuasively between his contradictor's eyes. The

Oranese bleeds magnificently amid the vociferations of a wild audience. Despite the repeated encouragements of the gallery and of my neighbor, despite the dauntless shouts of "Kill him!," "Floor him!," the insidious "Below the belt," "Oh, the referee missed that one!," the optimistic "He's pooped," "He can't take any more," nevertheless the man from Algiers is proclaimed the winner on points amid interminable catcalls. My neighbor, who is inclined to talk of sportsmanship, applauds ostensibly, while slipping to me in a voice made faint by so many shouts: "So that he won't be able to say *back there* that we of Oran are savages."

But throughout the audience, fights not included on the program have already broken out. Chairs are brandished, the police clear a path, excitement is at its height. In order to calm these good people and contribute to the return of silence, the "management," without losing a moment, commissions the loudspeaker to boom out "Sambre-et-Meuse." For a few minutes the audience has a really warlike look. Confused clusters of combatants and voluntary referees sway in the grip of policemen; the gallery exults and calls for the rest of the program with wild cries, cock-a-doodle-doo's, and mocking catcalls drowned in the irresistible flood from the military band.

But the announcement of the big fight is enough to restore calm. This takes place suddenly, without flourishes, just as actors leave the stage once the play is finished. With the greatest unconcern, hats are dusted off, chairs are put back in place, and without transition all faces assume the kindly expression of the respectable member of the audience who has paid for his ticket to a family concert.

The last fight pits a French champion of the Navy against an Oran boxer. This time the difference in reach is to the advantage of the latter. But his superiorities, during the first rounds, do not stir the crowd. They are sleeping off the effects of their first excitement; they are sobering up. They are still short of breath. If they applaud, there is no passion in it. They hiss without animosity. The audience is divided into two camps, as is appropriate in the interest of fairness. But each individual's choice obeys that indifference that

follows on great expenditures of energy. If the Frenchman holds his own, if the Oranese forgets that one
doesn't lead with the head, the boxer is bent under a
volley of hisses, but immediately pulled upright again
by a burst of applause. Not until the seventh round does
sport rise to the surface again, at the same time that the
real enthusiasts begin to emerge from their fatigue. The
Frenchman, to tell the truth, has touched the mat and,
eager to win back points, has hurled himself on his opponent. "What did I tell you?" said my neighbor; "it's
going to be a fight to the finish." Indeed, it *is* a fight to
the finish. Covered with sweat under the pitiless light,
both boxers open their guard, close their eyes as they
hit, shove with shoulders and knees, swap their blood,
and snort with rage. As one man, the audience has stood
up and punctuates the efforts of its two heroes. It
receives the blows, returns them, echoes them in a thousand hollow, panting voices. The same ones who had
chosen their favorite in indifference cling to their choice
through obstinacy and defend it passionately. Every
ten seconds a shout from my neighbor pierces my right
ear: "Go to it, gob; come on, Navy!" while another man
in front of us shouts to the Oranese: "*Anda! hombre!*"
The man and the gob go to it, and together with them,
in this temple of whitewash, iron, and cement, an
audience completely given over to gods with cauli-
flower ears. Every blow that gives a dull sound on the
shining pectorals echoes in vast vibrations in the very
body of the crowd, which, with the boxers, is making its
last effort.

In such an atmosphere a draw is badly received.
Indeed, it runs counter to a quite Manichean tendency
in the audience. There is good and there is evil, the
winner and the loser. One must be either right or wrong.
The conclusion of this impeccable logic is immediately
provided by two thousand energetic lungs accusing the
judges of being sold, or bought. But the gob has walked
over and embraced his rival in the ring, drinking in his
fraternal sweat. This is enough to make the audience,
reversing its view, burst out in sudden applause. My
neighbor is right: they are not savages.

The crowd pouring out, under a sky full of silence

and stars, has just fought the most exhausting fight. It keeps quiet and disappears furtively, without any energy left for post mortems. There is good and there is evil; that religion is merciless. The band of faithful is now no more than a group of black-and-white shadows disappearing into the night. For force and violence are solitary gods. They contribute nothing to memory. On the contrary, they distribute their miracles by the handful in the present. They are made for this race without past which celebrates its communions around the prize ring. These are rather difficult rites but ones that simplify everything. Good and evil, winner and loser. At Corinth two temples stood side by side, the temple of Violence and the temple of Necessity.

Monuments

For many reasons due as much to economics as to metaphysics, it may be said that the Oranese style, if there is one, forcefully and clearly appears in the extraordinary edifice called the Maison du Colon. Oran hardly lacks monuments. The city has its quota of imperial marshals, ministers, and local benefactors. They are found on dusty little squares, resigned to rain and sun, they too converted to stone and boredom. But, in any case, they represent contributions from the outside. In that happy barbary they are the regrettable marks of civilization.

Oran, on the other hand, has raised up her altars and rostra to her own honor. In the very heart of the mercantile city, having to construct a common home for the innumerable agricultural organizations that keep this country alive, the people of Oran conceived the idea of building solidly a convincing image of their virtues: the Maison du Colon. To judge from the edifice, those virtues are three in number: boldness in taste, love of violence, and a feeling for historical syntheses. Egypt, Byzantium, and Munich collaborated in the delicate construction of a piece of pastry in the shape of a bowl upside down. Multicolored stones, most vigorous in effect, have been brought in to outline the roof. These mosaics are so exuberantly persuasive that at first you see nothing but an amorphous effulgence. But with a closer view and your attention called to it, you discover that they have a meaning: a graceful colonist, wearing a bow tie and white pith helmet, is receiving the homage of a procession of slaves dressed in classical style.[4] The edifice and its colored illustrations have been set down in the middle of a square in the to-and-fro of the little two-car trams whose filth is one of the charms of the city.

Oran greatly cherishes also the two lions of its Place d'Armes, or parade ground. Since 1888 they have been sitting in state on opposite sides of the municipal stairs. Their author was named Cain. They have majesty and a stubby torso. It is said that at night they get down from their pedestal one after the other, silently pace around the dark square, and on occasion urinate at length under the big, dusty ficus trees. These, of course, are rumors to which the people of Oran lend an indulgent ear. But it is unlikely.

Despite a certain amount of research, I have not been able to get interested in Cain. I merely learned that he had the reputation of being a skillful animal-sculptor. Yet I often think of him. This is an intellectual bent that comes naturally in Oran. Here is a sonorously named artist who left an unimportant work here. Several hundred thousand people are familiar with the easy-going beasts he put in front of a pretentious town hall. This is one way of succeeding in art. To be sure, these two lions, like thousands of works of the same type, are proof of something else than talent. Others have created "The Night Watch," "Saint Francis Receiving the Stigmata," "David," or the Pharsalian bas-relief called "The Glorification of the Flower." Cain, on the other hand, set up two hilarious snouts on the square of a mercantile province overseas. But the David will go down one day with Florence and the lions will perhaps be saved from the catastrophe. Let me repeat, they are proof of something else.

Can one state this idea clearly? In this work there are insignificance and solidity. Spirit counts for nothing and matter for a great deal. Mediocrity insists upon

---

[4] Another quality of the Algerian race is, as you see, candor.

lasting by all means, including bronze. It is refused a
right to eternity, and every day it takes that right. Is it
not eternity itself? In any event, such perseverance is
capable of stirring, and it involves its lesson, that of all
the monuments of Oran, and of Oran herself. An hour
a day, every so often, it forces you to pay attention to
something that has no importance. The mind profits
from such recurrences. In a sense this is its hygiene, and
since it absolutely needs its moments of humility, it
seems to me that this chance to indulge in stupidity is
better than others. Everything that is ephemeral wants
to last. Let us say that everything wants to last. Human
productions mean nothing else, and in this regard Cain's
lions have the same chances as the ruins of Angkor.
This disposes one toward modesty.

There are other Oranese monuments. Or at least they
deserve this name because they, too, stand for their city,
and perhaps in a more significant way. They are the
public works at present covering the coast for some ten
kilometers. Apparently it is a matter of transforming the
most luminous of bays into a gigantic harbor. In reality
it is one more chance for man to come to grips with
stone.

In the paintings of certain Flemish masters a theme
of strikingly general application recurs insistently: the
building of the Tower of Babel. Vast landscapes, rocks
climbing up to heaven, steep slopes teeming with work-
men, animals, ladders, strange machines, cords, pulleys.
Man, moreover, is there only to give scale to the inhuman scope of the construction. This is what the Oran
coast makes one think of, west of the city.

Clinging to vast slopes, rails, dump-cars, cranes, tiny
trains . . . Under a broiling sun, toy-like locomotives
round huge blocks of stone amid whistles, dust, and
smoke. Day and night a nation of ants bustles about on
the smoking carcass of the mountain. Clinging all up
and down a single cord against the side of the cliff,
dozens of men, their bellies pushing against the handles
of automatic drills, vibrate in empty space all day long
and break off whole masses of rock that hurtle down in
dust and rumbling. Farther on, dump-carts tip their
loads over the slopes; and the rocks, suddenly poured

seaward, bound and roll into the water, each large lump followed by a scattering of lighter stones. At regular intervals, at dead of night or in broad daylight, detonations shake the whole mountain and stir up the sea itself.

Man, in this vast construction field, makes a frontal attack on stone. And if one could forget, for a moment at least, the harsh slavery that makes this work possible, one would have to admire. These stones, torn from the mountain, serve man in his plans. They pile up under the first waves, gradually emerge, and finally take their place to form a jetty, soon covered with men and machines which advance, day after day, toward the open sea. Without stopping, huge steel jaws bite into the cliff's belly, turn round, and disgorge into the water their overflowing gravel. As the coastal cliff is lowered, the whole coast encroaches irresistibly on the sea.

Of course, destroying stone is not possible. It is merely moved from one place to another. In any case, it will last longer than the men who use it. For the moment, it satisfies their will to action. That in itself is probably useless. But moving things about is the work of men; one must choose doing that or nothing.[5] Obviously the people of Oran have chosen. In front of that indifferent bay, for many years more they will pile up stones along the coast. In a hundred years—tomorrow, in other words—they will have to begin again. But today these heaps of rocks testify for the men in masks of dust and sweat who move about among them. The true monuments of Oran are still her stones.

Ariadne's Stone

It seems that the people of Oran are like that friend of Flaubert who, on the point of death, casting a last glance at this irreplaceable earth, exclaimed: "Close the window; it's too beautiful." They have closed the window, they have walled themselves in, they have cast out the landscape. But Flaubert's friend, Le Poittevin, died, and after him days continued to be added to days. Likewise, beyond the yellow walls of Oran, land and sea continue

[5] This essay deals with a certain temptation. It is essential to have known it. One can then act or not, but with full knowledge of the facts.

their indifferent dialogue. That permanence in the world has always had contrary charms for man. It drives him to despair and excites him. The world never says but one thing; first it interests, then it bores. But eventually it wins out by dint of obstinacy. It is always right.

Already, at the very gates of Oran, nature raises its voice. In the direction of Canastel there are vast waste-lands covered with fragrant brush. There sun and wind speak only of solitude. Above Oran there is the mountain of Santa-Cruz, the plateau and the myriad ravines leading to it. Roads, once carriageable, cling to the slopes overhanging the sea. In the month of January some are covered with flowers. Daisies and buttercups turn them into sumptuous paths, embroidered in yellow and white. About Santa-Cruz everything has been said. But if I were to speak of it, I should forget the sacred processions that climb the rugged hill on feast days, in order to recall other pilgrimages. Solitary, they walk in the red stone, rise above the motionless bay, and come to dedicate to nakedness a luminous, perfect hour.

Oran has also its deserts of sand: its beaches. Those encountered near the gates are deserted only in winter and spring. Then they are plateaus covered with aspho-dels, peopled with bare little cottages among the flowers. The sea rumbles a bit, down below. Yet already the sun, the faint breeze, the whiteness of the asphodels, the sharp blue of the sky, everything makes one fancy sum-mer—the golden youth then covering the beach, the long hours on the sand and the sudden softness of evening. Each year on these shores there is a new harvest of girls in flower. Apparently they have but one season. The following year, other cordial blossoms take their place, which, the summer before, were still little girls with bodies as hard as buds. At eleven A.M., coming down from the plateau, all that young flesh, lightly clothed in motley materials, breaks on the sand like a multicolored wave.

One has to go farther (strangely close, however, to that spot where two hundred thousand men are labor-ing) to discover a still virgin landscape: long, deserted dunes where the passage of men has left no other trace than a worm-eaten hut. From time to time an Arab shep-herd drives along the top of the dunes the black and beige spots of his flock of goats. On the beaches of the Oran country every summer morning seems to be the first in the world. Each twilight seems to be the last, solemn agony, announced at sunset by a final glow that darkens every hue. The sea is ultramarine, the road the color of clotted blood, the beach yellow. Everything disappears with the green sun; an hour later the dunes are bathed in moonlight. Then there are incomparable nights under a rain of stars. Occasionally storms sweep over them, and the lightning flashes flow along the dunes, whiten the sky, and give the sand and one's eyes orange-colored glints.

But this cannot be shared. One has to have lived it. So much solitude and nobility give these places an unforgettable aspect. In the warm moment before daybreak, after confronting the first bitter, black waves, a new creature breasts night's heavy, enveloping water. The memory of those joys does not make me regret them, and thus I recognize that they were good. After so many years they still last, somewhere in this heart which finds unswerving loyalty so difficult. And I know that today, if I were to go to the deserted dune, the same sky would pour down on me its cargo of breezes and stars. These are lands of innocence.

But innocence needs sand and stones. And man has forgotten how to live among them. At least it seems so, for he has taken refuge in this extraordinary city where boredom sleeps. Nevertheless, that very confrontation constitutes the value of Oran. The capital of boredom, besieged by innocence and beauty, it is surrounded by an army in which every stone is a soldier. In the city, and at certain hours, however, what a temptation to go over to the enemy! What a temptation to identify oneself with those stones, to melt into that burning and impassive universe that defies history and its ferments! That is doubtless futile. But there is in every man a profound instinct which is neither that of destruction nor that of creation. It is merely a matter of resembling nothing. In the shadow of the warm walls of Oran, on its dusty asphalt, that invitation is sometimes heard. It seems that, for a time, the minds that yield to it are never disappointed. This is the darkness of Eurydice and the sleep of Isis. Here are the deserts where thought will collect itself, the cool hand of evening on a troubled heart. On this Mount of Olives, vigil is futile; the mind recalls and approves the sleeping Apostles. Were they really wrong? They nonetheless had their revelation.

Just think of Sakyamuni in the desert. He remained there for years on end, squatting motionless with his eyes on heaven. The very gods envied him that wisdom and that stone-like destiny. In his outstretched hands the swallows had made their nest. But one day they flew away, answering the call of distant lands. And he who had stifled in himself desire and will, fame and suffering, began to cry. It happens thus that flowers grow on rocks. Yes, let us accept stone when it is necessary. That secret and that rapture we ask of faces can also be given us by stone. To be sure, this cannot last. But what *can* last, after all? The secret of faces fades away, and there we are, cast back to the chain of desires. And if stone can do no more for us than the human heart, at least it can do just as much.

"Oh, to be nothing!" For thousands of years this great cry has roused millions of men to revolt against desire and pain. Its dying echoes have reached this far, across centuries and oceans, to the oldest sea in the world. They still reverberate dully against the compact cliffs of Oran. Everybody in this country follows this advice without knowing it. Of course, it is almost futile. Nothingness cannot be achieved any more than the absolute can. But since we receive as favors the eternal signs brought us by roses or by human suffering, let us not refuse either the rare invitations to sleep that the earth addresses us. Each has as much truth as the other.

This, perhaps, is the Ariadne's thread of this somnambulist and frantic city. Here one learns the virtues, provisional to be sure, of a certain kind of boredom. In order to be spared, one must say "yes" to the Minotaur. This is an old and fecund wisdom. Above the sea, silent at the base of the red cliffs, it is enough to maintain a delicate equilibrium halfway between the two massive headlands which, on the right and left, dip into the clear water. In the puffing of a coast-guard vessel crawling along the water far out bathed in radiant light, is distinctly heard the muffled call of inhuman and glittering forces: it is the Minotaur's farewell.

It is noon; the very day is being weighed in the balance. His rite accomplished, the traveler receives the reward of his liberation: the little stone, dry and smooth as an asphodel, that he picks up on the cliff. For the initiate the world is no heavier to bear than this stone. Atlas's task is easy; it is sufficient to choose one's hour. Then one realizes that for an hour, a month, a year, these shores can indulge in freedom. They welcome pell-mell, without even looking at them, the monk, the civil servant, or the conqueror. There are days when I expected to meet, in the streets of Oran, Descartes or Cesare Borgia. That did not happen. But perhaps another will be more fortunate. A great deed, a great work, virile meditation used to call for the solitude of sands or of the convent. There were kept the spiritual vigils of arms. Where could they be better celebrated now than in the emptiness of a big city established for some time in unintellectual beauty?

Here is the little stone, smooth as an asphodel. It is at the beginning of everything. Flowers, tears (if you insist), departures, and struggles are for tomorrow. In the middle of the day when the sky opens its fountains of light in the vast, sonorous space, all the headlands of the coast look like a fleet about to set out. Those heavy galleons of rock and light are trembling on their keels as if they were preparing to steer for sunlit isles. O mornings in the country of Oran! From the high plateaus the swallows plunge into huge troughs where the air is seething. The whole coast is ready for departure; a shiver of adventure ripples through it. Tomorrow, perhaps, we shall leave together.

(1939)

Helen's Exile

✳

The Mediterranean sun has something tragic about it, quite different from the tragedy of fogs. Certain evenings at the base of the seaside mountains, night falls over the flawless curve of a little bay, and there rises from the silent waters a sense of anguished fulfillment. In such spots one can understand that if the Greeks knew despair, they always did so through beauty and its stifling quality. In that gilded calamity, tragedy reaches its highest point. Our time, on the other hand, has fed its despair on ugliness and convulsions. This is why Europe would be vile, if suffering could ever be so.

We have exiled beauty; the Greeks took up arms for her. First difference, but one that has a history. Greek thought always took refuge behind the conception of limits. It never carried anything to extremes, neither the sacred nor reason, because it negated nothing, neither the sacred nor reason. It took everything into consideration, balancing shadow with light. Our Europe, on the other hand, off in the pursuit of totality, is the child of disproportion. She negates beauty, as she negates whatever she does not glorify. And, through all her diverse ways, she glorifies but one thing, which is the future rule of reason. In her madness she extends the eternal limits, and at that very moment dark Erinyes fall upon her and tear her to pieces. Nemesis, the goddess of measure and not of revenge, keeps watch. All those who overstep the limit are pitilessly punished by her.

The Greeks, who for centuries questioned themselves as to what is just, could understand nothing of our idea of justice. For them equity implied a limit, whereas our whole continent is convulsed in its search for a justice that must be total. At the dawn of Greek thought Heraclitus was already imagining that justice sets limits for the physical universe itself: "The sun will not overstep his measures; if he does, the Erinyes, the handmaids of justice, will find him out." [1] We who have cast the universe and spirit out of our sphere laugh at that threat. In a drunken sky we light up the suns we want. But nonetheless the boundaries exist, and we know it. In our wildest aberrations we dream of an equilibrium we have left behind, which we naïvely expect to find at the end of our errors. Childish presumption which justifies the fact that child-nations, inheriting our follies, are now directing our history.

A fragment attributed to the same Heraclitus simply states: "Presumption, regression of progress." And, many centuries after the man of Ephesus, Socrates, facing the threat of being condemned to death, acknowledged only this one superiority in himself: what he did not know he did not claim to know. The most exemplary life and thought of those centuries close on a proud confession of ignorance. Forgetting that, we have forgotten our virility. We have preferred the power that apes greatness, first Alexander and then the Roman conquerors whom the authors of our schoolbooks, through some incomparable vulgarity, teach us to admire. We, too, have conquered, moved boundaries, mastered heaven and earth. Our reason has driven all away. Alone at last, we end up by ruling over a desert. What imagination could we have left for that higher equilibrium in which nature balanced history, beauty, virtue, and which applied the music of numbers even to blood-tragedy? We turn our backs on nature; we are ashamed of beauty. Our wretched tragedies have a smell of the office clinging to them, and the blood that trickles from them is the color of printer's ink.

This is why it is improper to proclaim today that we are the sons of Greece. Or else we are the renegade sons. Placing history on the throne of God, we are progressing toward theocracy like those whom the Greeks called Barbarians and whom they fought to death in the waters of Salamis. In order to realize how we differ, one must turn to him among our philosophers who is the true

[1] Bywater's translation. [Translator's note.]

rival of Plato. "Only the modern city," Hegel dares write, "offers the mind a field in which it can become aware of itself." We are thus living in the period of big cities. Deliberately, the world has been amputated of all that constitutes its permanence: nature, the sea, hilltops, evening meditation. Consciousness is to be found only in the streets, because history is to be found only in the streets—this is the edict. And consequently our most significant works show the same bias. Landscapes are not to be found in great European literature since Dostoevsky. History explains neither the natural universe that existed before it nor the beauty that exists above it. Hence it chose to be ignorant of them. Whereas Plato contained everything—nonsense, reason, and myth—our philosophers contain nothing but nonsense or reason because they have closed their eyes to the rest. The mole is meditating.

It is Christianity that began substituting the tragedy of the soul for contemplation of the world. But, at least, Christianity referred to a spiritual nature and thereby preserved a certain fixity. With God dead, there remains only history and power. For some time the entire effort of our philosophers has aimed solely at replacing the notion of human nature with that of situation, and replacing ancient harmony with the disorderly advance of chance or reason's pitiless progress. Whereas the Greeks gave to will the boundaries of reason, we have come to put the will's impulse in the very center of reason, which has, as a result, become deadly. For the Greeks, values pre-existed all action, of which they definitely set the limits. Modern philosophy places its values at the end of action. They *are* not but *are becoming*, and we shall know them fully only at the completion of history. With values, all limit disappears, and since conceptions differ as to what they will be, since all struggles, without the brake of those same values, spread indefinitely, today's Messianisms confront one another and their clamors mingle in the clash of empires. Disproportion is a conflagration, according to Heraclitus. The conflagration is spreading; Nietzsche is outdistanced. Europe no longer philosophizes by striking a hammer, but by shooting a cannon.

Nature is still there, however. She contrasts her calm skies and her reasons with the madness of men. Until the atom too catches fire and history ends in the triumph of reason and the agony of the species. But the Greeks never said that the limit could not be overstepped. They said it existed and that whoever dared to exceed it was mercilessly struck down. Nothing in present history can contradict them.

The historical spirit and the artist both want to remake the world. But the artist, through an obligation of his nature, knows his limits, which the historical spirit fails to recognize. This is why the latter's aim is tyranny whereas the former's passion is freedom. All those who are struggling for freedom today are ultimately fighting for beauty. Of course, it is not a question of defending beauty for itself. Beauty cannot do without man, and we shall not give our era its nobility and serenity unless we follow it in its misfortune. Never again shall we be hermits. But it is no less true that man cannot do without beauty, and this is what our era pretends to want to disregard. It steels itself to attain the absolute and authority; it wants to transfigure the world before having exhausted it, to set it to rights before having understood it. Whatever it may say, our era is deserting this world. Ulysses can choose at Calypso's bidding between immortality and the land of his fathers. He chooses the land, and death with it. Such simple nobility is foreign to us today. Others will say that we lack humility; but, all things considered, this word is ambiguous. Like Dostoevsky's fools who boast of everything, soar to heaven, and end up flaunting their shame in any public place, we merely lack man's pride, which is fidelity to his limits, lucid love of his condition.

"I hate my time," Saint-Exupéry wrote shortly before his death, for reasons not far removed from those I have spoken of. But, however upsetting that exclamation, coming from him who loved men for their admirable qualities, we shall not accept responsibility for it. Yet what a temptation, at certain moments, to turn one's back on this bleak, fleshless world! But this time is ours, and we cannot live hating ourselves. It has fallen so low only through the excess of its virtues as well as through the extent of its vices.

We shall fight for the virtue that has a history. What virtue? The horses of Patroclus weep for their master killed in battle. All is lost. But Achilles resumes the fight, and victory is the outcome, because friendship has just been assassinated: friendship is a virtue.

Admission of ignorance, rejection of fanaticism, the limits of the world and of man, the beloved face, and finally beauty—this is where we shall be on the side of the Greeks. In a certain sense, the direction history will take is not the one we think. It lies in the struggle between creation and inquisition. Despite the price which artists will pay for their empty hands, we may hope for their victory. Once more the philosophy of darkness will break and fade away over the dazzling sea. O midday thought, the Trojan war is being fought far from the battlefields! Once more the dreadful walls of the modern city will fall to deliver up—"soul serene as the ocean's calm"—the beauty of Helen.

(1948)

Return to Tipasa

You have navigated with raging soul far from the paternal home, passing beyond the sea's double rocks, and you now inhabit a foreign land.

MEDEA

For five days rain had been falling ceaselessly on Algiers and had finally wet the sea itself. From an apparently inexhaustible sky, constant downpours, viscous in their density, streamed down upon the gulf. Gray and soft as a huge sponge, the sea rose slowly in the ill-defined bay. But the surface of the water seemed almost motionless under the steady rain. Only now and then a barely perceptible swelling motion would raise above the sea's surface a vague puff of smoke that would come to dock in the harbor, under an arc of wet boulevards. The city itself, all its white walls dripping, gave off a different steam that went out to meet the first steam. Whichever way you turned, you seemed to be breathing water, to be drinking the air.

In front of the soaked sea I walked and waited in that December Algiers, which was for me the city of summers. I had fled Europe's night, the winter of faces. But the summer city herself had been emptied of her laughter and offered me only bent and shining backs. In the evening, in the crudely lighted cafés where I took refuge, I read my age in faces I recognized without being able to name them. I merely knew that they had been young with me and that they were no longer so.

Yet I persisted without very well knowing what I was waiting for, unless perhaps the moment to go back to Tipasa. To be sure, it is sheer madness, almost always punished, to return to the sites of one's youth and try to relive at forty what one loved or keenly enjoyed at twenty. But I was forewarned of that madness. Once already I had returned to Tipasa, soon after those war years that marked for me the end of youth. I hoped, I think, to recapture there a freedom I could not forget. In that spot, indeed, more than twenty years ago, I had spent whole mornings wandering among the ruins, breathing in the wormwood, warming myself against the stones, discovering little roses, soon plucked of their petals, which outlive the spring. Only at noon, at the hour when the cicadas themselves fell silent as if overcome, I would flee the greedy glare of an all-consuming light. Sometimes at night I would sleep open-eyed under a sky dripping with stars. I was alive then. Fifteen years later I found my ruins, a few feet from the first waves, I followed the streets of the forgotten walled city through fields covered with bitter trees, and on the slopes overlooking the bay I still caressed the bread-colored columns. But the ruins were now surrounded with barbed wire and could be entered only through certain openings. It was also forbidden, for reasons which it appears that morality approves, to walk there at night; by day one encountered an official guardian. It just happened, that morning, that it was raining over the whole extent of the ruins.

Disoriented, walking through the wet, solitary countryside, I tried at least to recapture that strength, hitherto always at hand, that helps me to accept *what is* when once I have admitted that I cannot change it. And I could not, indeed, reverse the course of time and restore to the world the appearance I had loved which had disappeared in a day, long before. The second of September 1939, in fact, I had not gone to Greece, as I was to do. War, on the contrary, had come to us, then it had spread over Greece herself. That distance, those years separating the warm ruins from the barbed wire were to be found in me, too, that day as I stood before the sarcophaguses full of black water or under the sodden tamarisks. Originally brought up surrounded by beauty which was my only wealth, I had begun in plenty. Then had come the barbed wire—I mean tyrannies, war, police forces, the era of revolt. One had had to put oneself right with the authorities of night: the day's beauty was but a memory. And in this muddy Tipasa the memory itself was becoming dim. It was indeed a question of beauty, plenty, or youth! In the light from conflagrations the world had suddenly shown its wrinkles and its wounds, old and new. It had aged all at once, and we with it. I had come here looking for a certain "lift"; but I realized that it inspires only the man who is unaware that he is about to launch forward. No love without a little innocence. Where was the innocence? Empires were tumbling down; nations and men were tearing at one another's throats; our hands were soiled. Originally innocent without knowing it, we were now guilty without meaning to be: the mystery was increasing with our knowledge. This is why, O mockery, we were concerned with morality. Weak and disabled, I was dreaming of virtue! In the days of innocence I didn't even know that morality existed. I knew it now, and I was not capable of living up to its standard. On the promontory that I used to love, among the wet columns of the ruined temple, I seemed to be walking behind someone whose steps I could still hear on the stone slabs and mosaics but whom I should never again overtake. I went back to Paris and remained several years before returning home.

Yet I obscurely missed something during all those years. When one has once had the good luck to love intensely, life is spent in trying to recapture that ardor and that illumination. Forsaking beauty and the sensual happiness attached to it, exclusively serving misfortune, calls for a nobility I lack. But, after all, nothing is true that forces one to exclude. Isolated beauty ends up simpering; solitary justice ends up oppressing. Whoever aims to serve one exclusive of the other serves no one, not even himself, and eventually serves injustice twice. A day comes when, thanks to rigidity, nothing causes wonder any more, everything is known, and life is spent in beginning over again. These are the days of exile, of desiccated life, of dead souls. To come alive again, one needs a special grace, self-forgetfulness, or a homeland. Certain mornings, on turning a corner, a delightful dew falls on the heart and then evaporates. But its coolness remains, and this is what the heart requires always. I had to set out again.

And in Algiers a second time, still walking under the

same downpour which seemed not to have ceased since a departure I had thought definitive, amid the same vast melancholy smelling of rain and sea, despite this misty sky, these backs fleeing under the shower, these cafés whose sulphureous light distorted faces, I persisted in hoping. Didn't I know, besides, that Algiers rains, despite their appearance of never meaning to end, nonetheless stop in an instant, like those streams in my country which rise in two hours, lay waste acres of land, and suddenly dry up? One evening, in fact, the rain ceased. I waited one night more. A limpid morning rose, dazzling, over the pure sea. From the sky, fresh as a daisy, washed over and over again by the rains, reduced by these repeated washings to its finest and clearest texture, emanated a vibrant light that gave to each house and each tree a sharp outline, an astonished newness. In the world's morning the earth must have sprung forth in such a light. I again took the road for Tipasa.

For me there is not a single one of those sixty-nine kilometers that is not filled with memories and sensations. Turbulent childhood, adolescent daydreams in the drone of the bus's motor, mornings, unspoiled girls, beaches, young muscles always at the peak of their effort, evening's slight anxiety in a sixteen-year-old heart, lust for life, fame, and ever the same sky throughout the years, unfailing in strength and light, itself insatiable, consuming one by one over a period of months the victims stretched out in the form of crosses on the beach at the deathlike hour of noon. Always the same sea, too, almost impalpable in the morning light, which I again saw on the horizon as soon as the road, leaving the Sahel and its bronze-colored vineyards, sloped down toward the coast. But I did not stop to look at it. I wanted to see again the Chenoua, that solid, heavy mountain cut out of a single block of stone, which borders the bay of Tipasa to the west before dropping down into the sea itself. It is seen from a distance, long before arriving, a light, blue haze still confused with the sky. But gradually it is condensed, as you advance toward it, until it takes on the color of the surrounding waters, a huge motionless wave whose amazing leap upward has been brutally solidified above the sea calmed all at once. Still nearer, almost at the gates of Tipasa, here is its frowning bulk, brown and green, here is the old mossy god that nothing will ever shake, a refuge and harbor for its sons, of whom I am one.

While watching it I finally got through the barbed wire and found myself among the ruins. And under the glorious December light, as happens but once or twice in lives which ever after can consider themselves favored to the full, I found exactly what I had come seeking, what, despite the era and the world, was offered me, truly to me alone, in that forsaken nature. From the forum strewn with olives could be seen the village down below. No sound came from it; wisps of smoke rose in the limpid air. The sea likewise was silent as if smothered under the unbroken shower of dazzling, cold light. From the Chenoua a distant cock's crow alone celebrated the day's fragile glory. In the direction of the ruins, as far as the eye could see, there was nothing but pock-marked stones and wormwood, trees and perfect columns in the transparence of the crystalline air. It seemed as if the morning were stabilized, the sun stopped for an incalculable moment. In this light and this silence, years of wrath and night melted slowly away. I listened to an almost forgotten sound within myself as if my heart, long stopped, were calmly beginning to beat again. And awake now, I recognized one by one the imperceptible sounds of which the silence was made up: the figured bass of the birds, the sea's faint, brief signs at the foot of the rocks, the vibration of the trees, the blind singing of the columns, the rustling of the wormwood plants, the furtive lizards. I heard that; I also listened to the happy torrents rising within me. It seemed to me that I had at last come to harbor, for a moment at least, and that henceforth that moment would be endless. But soon after, the sun rose visibly a degree in the sky. A magpie preluded briefly, and at once, from all directions, birds' songs burst out with energy, jubilation, joyful discordance, and infinite rapture. The day started up again. It was to carry me to evening.

At noon on the half-sandy slopes covered with heliotropes like a foam left by the furious waves of the last few days as they withdrew, I watched the sea barely swelling at that hour with an exhausted motion, and I satisfied the two thirsts one cannot long neglect without drying up—I mean loving and admiring. For there is merely bad luck in not being loved; there is misfortune in not loving. All of us, today, are dying of this misfortune. For violence and hatred dry up the heart itself; the long fight for justice exhausts the love that nevertheless gave birth to it. In the clamor in which we live, love is impossible and justice does not suffice. This is why Europe hates daylight and is only able to set injustice up against injustice. But in order to keep justice from shriveling up like a beautiful orange fruit containing nothing but a bitter, dry pulp, I discovered once more at Tipasa that one must keep intact in oneself a freshness, a cool wellspring of joy, love the day that escapes injustice, and return to combat having won that light. Here I recaptured the former beauty, a young sky, and I measured my luck, realizing at last that in the worst years of our madness the memory of that sky had never left me. This was what in the end had kept me from despairing. I had always known that the ruins of Tipasa were younger than our new constructions or our bomb damage. There the world began over again every day in an ever new light. O light! This is the cry of all the characters of ancient drama brought face to face with their fate. This last resort was ours, too, and I knew it now. In the middle of winter I at last discovered that there was in me an invincible summer.

I have again left Tipasa; I have returned to Europe and its struggles. But the memory of that day still uplifts me and helps me to welcome equally what delights and what crushes. In the difficult hour we are living, what else can I desire than to exclude nothing and to learn how to braid with white thread and black thread a single cord stretched to the breaking-point? In everything I have done or said up to now, I seem to recognize these two forces, even when they work at cross-purposes. I have not been able to disown the light into which I was born and yet I have not wanted to reject the servitudes of this time. It would be too easy to contrast here with the sweet name of Tipasa other more sonorous and crueler names. For men of today there is an inner way, which I know well from having taken it in both directions, leading from the spiritual hilltops to the capitals of crime. And doubtless one can always rest, fall asleep on the hilltop or board with crime. But if one forgoes a part of what is, one must forgo being oneself; one must forgo living or loving otherwise than by proxy. There is thus a will to live without rejecting anything of life, which is the virtue I honor most in this world. From time to time, at least, it is true that I should like to have practiced it. Inasmuch as few epochs require as much as ours that one should be equal to the best as to the worst, I should like, indeed, to shirk nothing and to keep faithfully a double memory. Yes, there is beauty and there are the humiliated. Whatever may be the difficulties of the undertaking, I should like never to be unfaithful either to one or to the others.

But this still resembles a moral code, and we live for something that goes farther than morality. If we could only name it, what silence! On the hill of Sainte-Salsa, to the east of Tipasa, the evening is inhabited. It is still light, to tell the truth, but in this light an almost invisible fading announces the day's end. A wind rises, young like the night, and suddenly the waveless sea chooses a direction and flows like a great barren river from one end of the horizon to the other. The sky darkens. Then begins the mystery, the gods of night, the beyond-pleasure. But how to translate this? The little coin I am carrying away from here has a visible surface, a woman's beautiful face which repeats to me all I have learned in this day, and a worn surface which I feel under my fingers during the return. What can that lipless mouth be saying, except what I am told by another mysterious voice, within me, which every day informs me of my ignorance and my happiness:

"The secret I am seeking lies hidden in a valley full of olive trees, under the grass and the cold violets, around an old house that smells of wood smoke. For more than twenty years I rambled over that valley and others resembling it, I questioned mute goatherds, I knocked at the door of deserted ruins. Occasionally, at the moment of the first star in the still bright sky, under a shower of shimmering light, I thought I knew. I did know, in truth. I still know, perhaps. But no one wants any of this secret; I don't want any myself, doubtless; and I cannot stand apart from my people. I live in my family, which thinks it rules over rich and hideous cities built of stones and mists. Day and night it speaks up, and everything bows before it, which bows before nothing: it is deaf to all secrets. Its power that carries me bores me, nevertheless, and on occasion its shouts weary me. But its misfortune is mine, and we are of the same blood. A cripple, likewise, an accomplice and noisy, have I not shouted among the stones? Consequently, I strive to forget, I walk in our cities of iron and fire, I smile bravely at the night, I hail the storms, I shall be faithful. I have forgotten, in truth: active and deaf, henceforth. But perhaps someday, when we are ready to die of exhaustion and ignorance, I shall be able to disown our garish tombs and go and stretch out in the valley, under the same light, and learn for the last time what I know."

(1952)

The Artist and
His Time

*

I. *As an artist, have you chosen the role of witness?*

This would take considerable presumption or a
vocation I lack. Personally I don't ask for any role and
I have but one real vocation. As a man, I have a preference
for happiness; as an artist, it seems to me that I still have
characters to bring to life without the help of wars or of
law-courts. But I have been sought out, as each individual
has been sought out. Artists of the past could at least keep
silent in the face of tyranny. The tyrannies of today are
improved; they no longer admit of silence or neutrality.
One has to take a stand, be either for or against. Well, in
that case, I am against.

But this does not amount to choosing the comfortable
role of witness. It is merely accepting the time as it is,
minding one's own business, in short. Moreover, you are
forgetting that today judges, accused, and witnesses exchange positions with exemplary rapidity. My choice, if
you think I am making one, would at least be never to
sit on a judge's bench, or beneath it, like so many of our
philosophers. Aside from that, there is no dearth of op-
portunities for action, in the relative. Trade-unionism is
today the first, and the most fruitful among them.

II. *Is not the quixotism that has been criticized in your
recent works an idealistic and romantic definition of the
artist's role?*

However words are perverted, they provisionally keep
their meaning. And it is clear to me that the romantic is

the one who chooses the perpetual motion of history, the grandiose epic, and the announcement of a miraculous event at the end of time. If I have tried to define something, it is, on the contrary, simply the common existence of history and of man, everyday life with the most possible light thrown upon it, the dogged struggle against one's own degradation and that of others.

It is likewise idealism, and of the worse kind, to end up by hanging all action and all truth on a meaning of history that is not implicit in events and that, in any case, implies a mythical aim. Would it therefore be realism to take as the laws of history the future—in other words, just what is not yet history, something of whose nature we know nothing?

It seems to me, on the contrary, that I am arguing in favor of a true realism against a mythology that is both illogical and deadly, and against romantic nihilism whether it be bourgeois or allegedly revolutionary. To tell the truth, far from being romantic, I believe in the necessity of a rule and an order. I merely say that there can be no question of just any rule whatsoever. And that it would be surprising if the rule we need were given us by this disordered society, or, on the other hand, by those doctrinaires who declare themselves liberated from all rules and all scruples.

III. *The Marxists and their followers likewise think they are humanists. But for them human nature will be formed in the classless society of the future.*

To begin with, this proves that they reject at the present moment what we all are: those humanists are accusers of man. How can we be surprised that such a claim should have developed in the world of court trials? They reject the man of today in the name of the man of the future. That claim is religious in nature. Why should it be more justified than the one which announces the kingdom of heaven to come? In reality the end of history cannot have, within the limits of our condition, any definable significance. It can only be the object of a faith and of a new mystification. A mystification that today is no less great than the one that of old based colonial oppression on the necessity of saving the souls of infidels.

IV. *Is not that what in reality separates you from the intellectuals of the left?*

You mean that is what separates those intellectuals from the left? Traditionally the left has always been at war against injustice, obscurantism, and oppression. It always thought that those phenomena were interdependent. The idea that obscurantism can lead to justice, the national interest to liberty, is quite recent. The truth is that certain intellectuals of the left (not all, fortunately) are today hypnotized by force and efficacy as our intellectuals of the right were before and during the war. Their attitudes are different, but the act of resignation is the same. The first wanted to be realistic nationalists; the second want to be realistic socialists. In the end they betray nationalism and socialism alike in the name of a realism henceforth without content and adored as a pure, and illusory, technique of efficacy.

This is a temptation that can, after all, be understood. But still, however the question is looked at, the new position of the people who call themselves, or think themselves, leftists consists in saying: certain oppressions are justifiable because they follow the direction, which cannot be justified, of history. Hence there are presumably privileged executioners, and privileged by nothing. This is about what was said in another context by Joseph de Maistre, who has never been taken for an incendiary. But this is a thesis which, personally, I shall always reject. Allow me to set up against it the traditional point of view of what has been hitherto called the left: all executioners are of the same family.

V. *What can the artist do in the world of today?*

He is not asked either to write about co-operatives or, conversely, to lull to sleep in himself the sufferings endured by others throughout history. And since you have asked me to speak personally, I am going to do so as simply as I can. Considered as artists, we perhaps have no need to interfere in the affairs of the world. But considered as men, yes. The miner who is exploited or shot down, the slaves in the camps, those in the colonies, the legions of persecuted throughout the world—they need all those who can speak to communicate their silence and to keep in touch with them. I have not written, day after day, fighting articles and texts, I have not taken part in the common struggles because I desire the world to be covered with Greek statues and masterpieces. The man who has such a desire does exist in me. Except that he has something better to do in trying to instill life into the creatures of his imagination. But from my first articles to my latest book I have written so much, and perhaps too much, only because I cannot keep from being drawn toward everyday life, toward those, whoever they may be, who are humiliated and debased. They need to hope, and if all keep silent or if they are given a choice between two kinds of humiliation, they will be forever deprived of hope and we with them. It seems to me impossible to endure that idea, nor can he who cannot endure it lie down to sleep in his tower. Not through virtue, as you see, but through a sort of almost organic intolerance, which you feel or do not feel. Indeed, I see many who fail to feel it, but I cannot envy their sleep.

This does not mean, however, that we must sacrifice our artist's nature to some social preaching or other. I have said elsewhere why the artist was more than ever necessary. But if we intervene as men, that experience will have an effect upon our language. And if we are not artists in our language first of all, what sort of artists are we? Even if, militants in our lives, we speak in our works of deserts and of selfish love, the mere fact that our lives are militant causes a special tone of voice to people with men that desert and that love. I shall certainly not choose the moment when we are beginning to leave nihilism behind to stupidly deny the values of creation in favor of the values of humanity, or vice versa. In my mind neither one is ever separated from the other and I measure the greatness of an artist (Molière, Tolstoy, Melville) by the balance he managed to maintain between the two. Today, under the pressure of events, we are obliged to transport that tension into our lives likewise.

This is why so many artists, bending under the burden, take refuge in the ivory tower or, conversely, in the social church. But as for me, I see in both choices a like act of resignation. We must simultaneously serve suffering and beauty. The long patience, the strength, the secret cunning such service calls for are the virtues that establish the very renascence we need.

One word more. This undertaking, I know, cannot be accomplished without dangers and bitterness. We must accept the dangers: the era of chairbound artists is over. But we must reject the bitterness. One of the temptations of the artist is to believe himself solitary, and in truth he hears this shouted at him with a certain base delight. But this is not true. He stands in the midst of all, in the same rank, neither higher nor lower, with all those who are working and struggling. His very vocation, in the face of oppression, is to open the prisons and to give a voice to the sorrows and joys of all. This is where art, against its enemies, justifies itself by proving precisely that it is no one's enemy. By itself art could probably not produce the renascence which implies justice and liberty. But without it, that renascence would be without forms and, consequently, would be nothing. Without culture, and the relative freedom it implies, society, even when perfect, is but a jungle. This is why any authentic creation is a gift to the future.

(*1953*)

ALBERT CAMUS *was born in Mondovi, Algeria, in 1913. After winning a degree in philosophy, he worked at various jobs, ending up in journalism. In the thirties, he ran a theatrical company, and during the war was active in the French Resistance, editing an important underground paper,* Combat. *Among his major works are four widely praised works of fiction,* The Stranger *(1946),* The Plague *(1948),* The Fall *(1957), and* Exile and the Kingdom *(1958); a volume of plays,* Caligula and Three Other Plays *(1958); and two books of philosophical essays,* The Rebel *(1954) and the pieces in this volume. Albert Camus was awarded the Nobel Prize for Literature in 1957. Both* The Stranger *and* The Rebel *are also available in the Vintage Series.*